An
Alignment
of Spirit

FINDING WORK YOU LOVE

MICHELLE WALTERS

LUMINOUS MOON PRESS
BOULDER, COLORADO

Published by Luminous Moon Press, LLC, Boulder, CO

Cover and interior layout and design by Carolyn Oakley,
Luminous Moon Design + Press | luminousmoon.com

First Edition
First Printing: May 2022

Publication Data
Michelle Walters
An Alignment of Spirit: Finding Work You Love

ISBN-13: 978-1-7372637-2-2

BUSINESS & ECONOMICS / Careers / Job Hunting — BODY,
MIND & SPIRIT / Inspiration & Personal Growth — BUSINESS &
ECONOMICS / Motivational

Printed and bound in the United States of America

ACKNOWLEDGMENTS

Writing this book has been a joy and an effort. It is the synthesis of many years of life experience and study. Many of those experiences have been wonderful and fulfilling, while others have humbled me and taught me about loss and grief.

So many people have contributed to making me who I am, and given me the life experiences and support to envision, compose, and produce this book. I want to begin by thanking several people who are deceased.

First, my husband Bruce. Bruce's optimism, determination and strong work ethic rubbed off on me. He brought an old soul wisdom to my life, and loved me with unshakable devotion. Bruce's "live for the moment" energy was inspiring and ever present. Thank you Bruce.

Second, my life partner Scott. Scott was the man of my dreams who loved me and supported me through many ups and downs. We shared so many passions including music, camping and how the mind works. Most of this book was composed while I worked in an office in Scott's house while he tried to recover from a stroke. Unfortunately Scott did not have a chance to read my book before he died. Thank you Scott.

Karen Gresham Nickell was my therapist, teacher and inspiration for multiple decades. A gifted psychic and empath, Karen stood by me through thick and thin, helping me see things from a higher perspective even when I felt like the world was crashing down on me. Karen's husband Robert watched my son Noah when he was a toddler so I could receive her help and teaching after Bruce's stroke. It is through connections of Karen's I met after her death I found the perfect team to help me publish my book. Thank you Karen.

Thank you to Michelle, my editor, and Carolyn, my publisher. My book would have likely sat on a digital shelf were it not for your help bringing this project to fruition. Thank you to my former boss, Debbie. Debbie has always been there for me and I deeply appreciate her input, understanding, and advice.

I am deeply grateful to my business coach, Caterina Rando. Caterina's enthusiasm and passion are a constant source of energy and encouragement.

My family has been important to me throughout my life, my sisters Desiree and Lynessa and my mother Carolyn. Thank you Carol, my stepmom, for reading and editing an early version of my book. No one has been more supportive to me than my Dad. In his older years he has bloomed and his generosity and love are incomparable. Thank you Daddy.

I have a cadre of girlfriends who have stood by me. There are too many to name them all, but I want to give a special shout out to Holly, Ida, Lisa, Lana, Karin, and Diana. They have listened to my tears, come to my parties, hugged me, walked with me, and held my hand. Thank you ladies.

My book about finding wonderful work would not exist without the many, many bosses, clients and colleagues I have worked with over the course of my career. I have learned so much from all of you. Thank you all for taking a chance on me and giving me the opportunity to contribute, learn, and grow. Thank you for the experience that enabled me to bring this book into being.

Thank you to Cinthia, whose teaching, love and passion have inspired and helped me find my way during turbulent times. Cinthia's generosity and drive for positive change often feel limitless. Thank you Cinthia for your deep empathy, strong intuition and practical guidance.

ACKNOWLEDGMENTS

Thank you to my son Noah. My life's greatest work and meaning has come from being Noah's Mom. I appreciate Noah's patience, resilience and support. Thank you for your love and for believing in me.

Thank you to my readers and followers. I hope that this book demonstrates the power of the mind and the importance of optimism and positive thinking. I fervently believe that there are too many people who overlook the spiritual significance of work and their jobs, and that this book can improve and accelerate their job hunt. Thank you for opening your mind.

AN ALIGNMENT OF SPIRIT: FINDING WORK YOU LOVE

CONTENTS

INTRODUCTION

WORK HAS A SPIRITUAL PURPOSE

Work most certainly does have a spiritual purpose. Approaching work, especially finding work, with anything less than a spiritually-aligned approach is unlikely to result in a job you love and a workplace where your spirit can truly take flight.

Finding a job is not for the faint of heart. How do I know? I've been there. In the last 20 years, I have found and received more than 18 new jobs. Incorporating spiritual practices into my job hunt has been critical to my success in finding those jobs.

What I want for you, as a job hunter or maybe a person looking for talent for your company, is to find and create work that is meaningful to your soul. I want to help you incorporate a spiritual side to your job hunt. Now is the time to begin to look at work differently than we have been taught. Enormous global changes will take place over the next twenty plus years. The advent of Artificial Intelligence is going to change what work looks like for millions of people, freeing them from tasks they do today and necessitating new tasks in the future. As I write this book in 2022, the world is still working to end a global pandemic. Working from home has become a new norm. There is a strong likelihood that office work and education as we knew it in 2019 will be gone, causing changes in commutes, real estate, and schools. Our planet cannot take much more in the way of manmade carbon emissions without disrupting earthly treasures we hold dear. Even now, polar bears, coral reefs, the Gulf Stream, and beaches are disappearing. The jobs organizations will be hiring for will need to shift if we want to preserve what we have.

In short, there have been a lot of changes and more will come. Now is the time to address those changes and the whole world of work and finding new work as part of a spiritual path and a spiritual life. The best time to learn how to approach your job hunt is now, using techniques that align the inner you with your new job.

IN THE BEGINNING

"Create a life that feels good on the inside
not just one that looks good on the outside."
— Billy Crystal

Changing our approach to work from only pragmatic to including a spiritual side needs to start with some definitions. The first word we need to define and clarify is the word spirituality itself. Definitions of spirituality span a wide range. Paul Gibbons, a business leader, author and keynote speaker, defines spirituality as "Growing and striving for meaning, purpose, goodness, and connectedness." The Royal College of Psychiatrists says, "Spirituality involves the recognition of a feeling or sense or belief that there is something greater than myself, something more to being human than sensory experience, and that the greater whole of which we are part is cosmic or divine in nature." In a paper published by the *Journal of Religion and Health*, a consortium of authors from a variety of disciplines described spirituality as, "One's striving for and experience of connection with oneself, connectedness with others and nature, and connectedness with the transcendent." Some definitions emphasize humanity; others emphasize the transcendent, sacred or divine

In Paul Gibbons' book, *The Spirituality of Work and Leadership*, he outlines three types of spirituality: secular, religious and mystical. Spirituality may be viewed through any of these lenses. I look at spirituality as a mix of all three. You may be more drawn to one type of spirituality more than another at any given point in your life. This book will work for you wherever you are at this moment. This brings us around to why many people, particularly business people, ask "Why should I incorporate spirituality in my job hunt? It can't be easily defined let alone measured." Business people, ever the pragmatists, tend to stick with concrete definitions and specific measurements.

However, in the case of the life of the spirit, the definitions are not nearly as important as the reality of what goes on in a job hunt. Once you are clear how much of what you are undertaking is happening in this realm we are calling spiritual, you will be much more clear how it creates and changes outcomes.

There are two main reasons why spirituality belongs in a job hunt. First, you have a subconscious that is making choices for you all the time. I place that subconscious firmly in the realm of the spiritual. We cannot define it, we know it impacts us, and we would like to be working in tandem with it, not against it. Working *with* the subconscious versus ignoring it will be more effective. Second, incorporating a spiritual component into your job hunt improves the whole experience. I have found that connecting with my spirit by taking the time and effort to access my subconscious mind as my partner and ally, accelerates and simplifies my job hunt as well as opens unexpected doors.

Our conscious mind is our critical mind. It consists of all our thoughts and experiences. The conscious mind is attuned to reason, evidence, and things we can observe. Obviously we can all see the benefit to working with the conscious mind when we are searching for jobs. However, when we focus solely on the conscious mind, we frequently ignore our experience of the subconscious and spirit.

Even when we are in our conscious mind, our subconscious mind is running all the time. It is in charge of our parasympathetic nervous system, which operates our physical system without us ever having to give it a thought. Take breathing as an example. Sure, you can be conscious about your breathing, but not always. You breathe even when you are not consciously thinking about it because your subconscious instructs your body to do so. Likewise, you digest food, you sweat, and you circulate your blood without ever using conscious thought.

When you tap the subconscious mind to be your partner and ally in your job hunt, all kinds of things happen. Here's an example. A friend of mine, someone I met socially who I've always held in high regard professionally, is someone I talk to or see maybe once a year. At one time, I was looking for a job and had been thinking about people who I thought might be able to help. She was one of these people.

It had been a long time since I had spoken to her, even though I thought about her at least weekly. This job hunt was a particularly difficult one, as I had suffered an enormous personal loss earlier that year. To my surprise, that very same friend reached out one day and let me know that a former employer of mine, one I had really admired, was looking for someone with my skill set locally. I reached out to them, interviewed and got the job.

Skeptics will say that my good fortune, this synchronicity, was not attributable to something coming from the mind or spirit, but instead due to facts we can consciously articulate. "The friend knew Michelle might be needing work after such a big loss and proactively reached out," they might say. That's one way of looking at it. My way holds more space for the connections between people and the ways in which the spirit moves through us. In the end we can't know for certain how that job came to me. However, this kind of synchronicity has happened to me so many times, I am confident there are thoughts and energies going on all the time; these energies are invisible and can be influenced by believing in them. Incorporating a spiritual perspective that harnesses the power of the subconscious in your job hunt is just plain smart.

Clearly, accessing your spirit and your subconscious alone will not bring you a job. We live in a universe made of matter and populated with other people who all have their own sense of self and experiences. Action on the physical plane is absolutely necessary accompanied by the help of our conscious and subconscious minds

Landing a job will come as a result of doing the spiritual work in harmony with the conscious actions you take. Over-focusing on conscious actions leaves out the spiritual side of things. It is also true that there are some people who may be more inclined to "pray for a job" and fail to take the conscious actions that lead to a job. Don't over focus on either side. Take a balanced approach and you will see results.

The Spiritual Purpose of Work

"Do or do not. There is no try." — Yoda

Our neglect in understanding how work fits into our spiritual path has misshaped thousands of people's careers and job hunts. As a society, we have become so focused on work absent its spiritual element, that our work lives and our personal lives are suffering.

Most of us have come to see the work as what we do for a paycheck, to feed our families, or to buy tickets to games or festivals or shows. We spend little or no time recognizing that our professional lives are a major part of our spiritual experience for our time here on earth.

The spiritual purpose of work is different for different people. It varies because we have different goals in each of our lives. It varies because even within the same person, your goals can be different at different times in your life. When it comes to spiritual paths, there's not so much a right and a wrong path. There is, however, a difference between moving and standing still.

There are at least six different spiritual purposes of work:

- **Growing**: The Challenges of Work, Growing From New Skills
- **Expressing**: Oneself From Your Place of True Self
- **Training**: Learning and Preparing For Something Else
- **Playing**: Making Work Feel Like Play
- **Interacting**: With Other People and Making the Lives of Others Better
- **Energizing**: Playing Your Part in the Flow of the Universe

How will you remember this? Try the acronym **GET PIE**. Who doesn't like pie?

Many people have more than one spiritual purpose of work, and it's possible to have all of these reasons. Here's a little bit more about each reason.

Growing: The Challenges of Work, Growing From New Skills

All work presents challenges. While some challenges are independent ones that teach us more about ourselves as an individual, increasingly many of us have jobs where we face challenges as a group. The experience of your team facing a deadline is not the same as when you face a deadline alone. As our society has evolved to having very large companies and millions of people in the workplace, the opportunities for spiritual growth for us as groups have expanded. In today's society where many people change jobs often and teams can be very fluid, the opportunities for spiritual growth of this type are enormous. Changing jobs frequently is likely to become more normal as the pace of change in our society continues to accelerate.

Just about every job will change from one year to the next. Almost no one is doing the exact same thing as they were even a year ago. Technologies change. Companies change. Mission statements change. Employees change. If you run your own business, you will constantly be needing to adapt to new ways of doing things. We all grow from learning new skills at work.

The individual skills we use at work may or may not appear to carry spiritual energy. Take the example of changing from managing email in Outlook to managing email in Google. I am hard pressed to see a tremendous difference at a spiritual level in changing your email tool. However, what goes along with the change inside of you may indeed carry spiritual value.

In the process of switching to Gmail, you may have to listen to new teachers. This could affect your respect for new people and how you treat others. You could also find the switch easier than you thought, increasing your self confidence and sense of self. You could find the new system easier and faster to manage, freeing some of your time and making your day go a little smoother. While new skills may not directly cause spiritual growth, they can indirectly cause or support spiritual growth.

Expressing: Oneself From Your Place of True Self

We are on this planet to explore who we are as humans. We grow in that exploration process. Each of us has our individual strengths, our weaknesses, and our unique opportunities. Work is a forum for us to express who we are, try things out, and explore. At work, we learn about our likes and dislikes, how to excel and how to fail, as well as how we do or don't set boundaries for ourselves. In the course of our lives, work is one of the biggest arenas in our exploration, expression, and definition of self. We spend so much time working and all workplaces have challenges, providing opportunities for exploration and growth.

Training: Learning and Preparing For Something Else

While the word of many spiritual advisors is to "live in the present," sometimes the present must be about training and preparing for the future. One experience we all have where our work is about preparing for the future is school. Depending on your profession, your schooling and training may be highly similar to your work or not. For example, if you are an apprentice, a beautician, or a welder, your work is likely very similar to your training. If you are a lawyer or a corporate writer, your training and your work may differ in significant ways.

When I went to graduate school in business, I had several classmates who wanted to work in the corporate office of a local prestigious outdoor goods retailer. This retailer had a rule that no one was hired by the corporate office without having spent some time working the floor in a retail job. It was critical to the firm's management that all personnel at their corporate office have experience in customer service, seeing the business through the eyes of a retail worker. While I had classmates who would have preferred to make the jump straight from graduate school to the corporate offices, the necessary loop through the retail environment made sure that everyone had some common experience and was truly committed to the organization. Sometimes the job you want will require preparation. And sometimes you will find that your job now is the perfect training ground for the next job you find.

Playing: Making Work Feel Like Play

Some people are lucky enough to find work so natural to their being that work feels like play. While having work feel like play may be an aspiration for some, having at least part of your day feel like play is an excellent goal. When work feels like play, it is easy, comes naturally, and is fun.

Finding work that feels like play is an example of when your spiritual alignment with work is at or near its maximum. If your work doesn't feel like play, ask yourself why not? What could you be doing that would feel better, and bring more joy into your life?

Few of us will find everything we do at work fun and enjoyable 100 percent of the time, but many of us can find more joy in our work than we do at the present moment. Believing that work can feel more like play is a good first step in aligning spirit with work.

Interacting: With Other People and Making the Lives of Others Better

Some people work primarily for the joy of being with others. Every human on earth has a spiritual journey which in some part is about learning from interacting with other humans. Granted, some journeys are more solo than others — the life of an Antarctic researcher probably has fewer social interactions than a concert promoter — but we all have to work with other people to some degree. For some people, interacting with other people is a means of spiritual growth and purpose.

A large number of people work because they are spiritually uplifted by how their work directly or indirectly helps others. Teachers, doctors, and air traffic controllers all play a part in growing, healing, and protecting others. It can be incredibly rewarding to serve other people and make the lives of our friends, neighbors and community better.

Energizing: Playing Your Part in the Flow of the Universe

Work is a major way the energy of the universe keeps moving. If everyone were just to stay home and stand still, the energetic flow of the Universe would be decreased. You are in the world of work to do all the things listed above and so is everyone you meet. Knowing that one simple fact will help you feel very differently about your job.

ϩ

This book will teach you how to get in touch with your spirit, using a variety of techniques largely centered on self-hypnosis. Accessing your inner wisdom via your subconscious is the means to attract work experiences that you find spiritually fulfilling.

How We Got Here

*"We have grasped the mystery of the atom and rejected the
Sermon on the Mount."* — Omar Bradley

The history of humanity and our relationship with the material
and the spiritual is a tale that veers one way and then the other.
Reflection on "how we got here" is helpful to understand where
we've been, where we are, and where we are going. A brief history of
spirituality is important to put everything in context.

Ancient civilizations, such as the aboriginals of Australia, held
beliefs called anima. These cultures, a few of which still exist today,
believe in a world that consists of the physical waking world and the
invisible spiritual world. For thousands of years, tribal life included a
strong attachment to the world of spirit, in parallel with the physical
world of our waking days.

Mankind's anima beliefs shifted from this balanced approach
to a more spiritual approach with the advent of polytheism and
monotheism. In polytheism, cultures viewed their Gods as having
a presence on the physical earth, and walking, at least some of the
time, among humanity. This shifted as polytheism was replaced by
monotheism. In monotheistic cultures, God was seen as an off-world,
heavenly being, who reigned over our physical earth.

As science developed, humanity became more and more interested
in our physical world. Bacon, Galileo, and Darwin were amongst the
many scientists who paved the way for a gradual shift away from our
previous monotheistic focus back toward a more material-based world.
The decline of religion over the last century is further testament to
humanity's current paradigm of heightened materialism.

Bhaerman and Lipton argue in *Spontaneous Evolution: Our Positive
Future and a Way to Get There From Here* that we are now moving
back towards a midpoint in the balance of spirit and materialism.
As evidence of this, they cite the Human Genome Project (HGP).
Scientists had predicted that in sequencing the Human Genome,

we would find 100,000 genes. However, when the enormous HGP project was completed, we discovered only 23,000 genes. What we came to realize was that we have many fewer genes than predicted. Other mechanisms, including physical experience or spirit, must be the catalyst for which genes are expressed and which are not.

The American workplace remains steeped in a high degree of materialism even though there is more going on under the surface than people are willing to recognize. While there is a global awakening and refreshed interest and focus on spirituality, we still have a long way to go. This book is meant to help us take a tiny step forward on that path.

In the United States and many western countries, our societies have evolved to make a strong distinction between the visible and the invisible, hard and soft skills, and spirit and matter. Descartes put us on a path of dividing the world into a materialistic one and a spiritual one, and humans have spent centuries living most of the time in that separation. I believe it is time to question that path and seek new answers.

SPIRITUALITY IN CORPORATE AMERICA

"Be the change you wish to see in the world." — Mahatma Ghandi

While Bhaerman and Lipton take a macro view of our evolutionary history, Ian Mitroff and Elizabeth Denton researched a smaller view. Ian Mitroff was the Harold Quinton Distinguished Professor of Business Policy at the Marshall School of Business at the University of Southern California. Elizabeth Denton is an Organizational Counseling Psychologist, Executive Coach and Strategic Consultant working in Tennessee. They studied spirituality in corporate America at the turn of the millennium. Their findings reveal further evidence that there is a significant gap in how individuals feel they can express themselves while at work in corporate America.

Mitroff and Denton point out in *A Spiritual Audit of Corporate America* that "our souls require proper nourishment to thrive."

We all know the importance of our feelings, our passion and our energy. Indeed, these characteristics are all part of our spiritual selves that uniquely define us as individuals and that we are meant to experience in our earthly lives.

In a comprehensive study consisting of 215 mailed questionnaires and in-depth interviews, Mitroff and Denton compiled a quantitative and qualitative perspective on the state of spirituality in corporate America. They found most organizations, both for-profit and not-for-profit, do not acknowledge the concept of spirituality or soul.

This lack of acknowledgement evidences a duality in the positions of many organizations. Many organizations call for unbridled energy and enthusiasm towards the work they demand from their workers. And yet, that energy and passion are elements of spirituality that the organizations don't even acknowledge. Mitroff and Denton found that many organizations have a "park it at the door" perspective on encouraging employees to express their spiritual nature at work.

While the definitions of spirituality varied widely across their survey respondents, there were a number of key findings in their study. I am highlighting some of these findings here; perhaps some of these will resonate with you.

Their survey respondents said spirituality is:

- Informal, structured, or organized like conventional religion.
- Non denominational and is inclusive. Everyone is included.
- Universal and timeless.
- The most important source of meaning and purpose in our lives.
- The idea that everything is sacred and interconnected.
- Founded on a deep faith, extraordinary willpower, and deeply connected to inner peace and calm.

Mitroff and Denton were particularly interested in understanding if respondents felt the ability to bring their entire selves to work. They felt this approach to spiritual inclusiveness would be understood by corporate America. If employees felt comfortable enough to bring their whole selves to work, they would be contributing all they had to their work efforts.

Survey respondents said they felt that their intelligence and creativity were welcome at work, but their feelings, soul, and humor were not. A decisive majority of respondents wanted to be comfortable expressing their full self at work but couldn't, given the tone and expectations of their workplace.

In summary, Mitroff and Denton believe that there is a clear need for a positive and greater role for spirituality in the corporate America workplace. Without additional focus on creating organizations and jobs that enable workers to express their full selves, we are limiting not just our human experience, but also what talents and strengths we bring to our work.

ME AND MY EXPERTISE

"Life is a banquet and most poor suckers are starving to death. Live!"
–– Auntie Mame

I am Michelle Walters and I am a lot of things. I'm a mom, a widow, a speaker, a consultant, a hypnotherapist, a daughter, a sister, and a friend. Besides being a former marketing executive and a current hypnotherapist and executive coach, I am also a seasoned job hunter.

For the last 20 plus years, I have been riding the wave of digital marketing. After finishing my MBA at the University of Washington in Seattle in 1997, I found myself on a career journey based on database and digital marketing that continued for over 20 years. I have had great fortune getting to work with big brands, small start-ups, and wise and bold entrepreneurs as my industry evolved from simple emails to websites, online advertising, social media, and more.

The primary theme over this time period has been change: technology has changed, companies have changed, people's skill sets have changed, and budgets have changed. All these variables are on a path to continue changing into the distant future. Pair this continual change with my natural curiosity, my inherent need for new things and plenty of instability in the market, and you have a recipe for a constant stream of new assignments and new jobs. Said another way, my spirit lives deep in the exploration zone. I want to share my experience with you so that you can be more spiritually fulfilled at work.

What I've learned is that it's important to keep yourself fresh, to market yourself, and to stay up-to-date on the latest developments in your industry and technology. But that is not enough. To get a job, to advance in your career, an alignment of spirit is necessary.

Why? Why is calling your co-workers, emailing resumés, or attending career fairs not enough? Because we are not on earth to exclusively experience reason and matter in the most pragmatic state. We are also here to learn that there are invisible forces outside of our control. We are here to explore our spirit and sometimes that means that a job that you consciously think is your next step, is not what the Universe has in mind. If that's the case, invisible forces will point you in a different direction and you can say goodbye to that job. Getting a job or making a career advancement is a spiritual experience. Approaching your job hunt without recognizing the spiritual nature of work means you are overlooking and missing the point of a major way to spend your life.

I know this from two sides — personal experience and professional exploration. As I mentioned, I have changed jobs numerous times over the last 20 years. Some of those changes were initiated directly by me and some were not. Many times I learned everything I needed to and I was done, and other times the outside circumstances changed and so the job was done. Regardless of how the change came to be, the point was that the job I was doing was no longer a good spiritual match for me, so the Universe changed up the game to make new and different opportunities appear.

With hindsight, I can make this sound like an easy process, but in going through it, it absolutely wasn't. Many times I found myself between things, and while I did make the best of that time, it was stressful and uncertain. To add to my stress, my husband was an extremely loving man, but physically unwell. He became severely disabled when my son was three and passed four years later, leaving me a single mom. Going through constant change on the career front is difficult when raising a kid by yourself. Ten years later, in 2021, after finding a wonderful new partner and getting engaged, my life partner suffered a stroke and seizures and died unexpectedly. This kind of challenge on the personal front takes an extreme toll on one's professional career.

I've been a student of the mind all my life and a hypnotherapist for the last several years. While we have so much more to learn from the esoteric sciences, there are a few metaphysical concepts that have stood the test of time. I believe like attracts like, and that you can, through your mindset and actions, draw on invisible forces to help you get a job. And I believe these skills are teachable and learnable.

When it comes to matters of the brain and mind, there are a lot of voices. This book draws from the work of social scientists, religious leaders, cognitive behaviorists and other teachers. It is important to do the work to both explore things from the inside out (leading with the subconscious) as well as the outside in (leading with the conscious). There is not one exact way to match your spirit with your work; there are many. This book seeks to engage both levels of the mind, the conscious and the subconscious, in order to align and attract work that is meaningful to you.

My Approach to Job Hunting

Over the course of my many job hunts, I have come to realize a few things: it is important to walk the walk, to take the steps and actions to get a job. Jobs can land in your lap, but that is seldom the case. The Universe delivers to the people who are taking action. All spirit and no action is a poor game plan.

In all cases, the energy you put into something is correlated with the energy that you get out of something. If you want a job, you need to put energy into it. Where my approach varies from that of other career advisors is that I advocate a balance of energy going into the nuts and bolts of getting a job *along with* energy going into the spiritual side of getting a job. Most advice on job hunting neglects the spiritual side.

Jobs arrive when they arrive. There are things you can do to spiritually prepare yourself and position yourself for jobs, but no matter how much you want to control the timeline, you really can't. It's true. If you are creating your own job you may have more influence over the timing than if you are employed by someone else, but even if you are self-employed, your work is a dance with the Universe and you are not the only dancer. Recognize you are an influencer of the timeline, not a controller. We will explore this more in future chapters.

What if we were to change the lens on our camera to look at things differently? What if instead of strictly following the current best practices for LinkedIn, we were to apply a spiritual approach to our career and job hunt? What if we thought about this not as what words will trigger a read of your resumé, but what your spirit is hungering for — nutritious, spirit-satisfying food? What if you were free enough to express your true nature at work and understood the growth of your spirit in the context of work?

WILL THIS BOOK HELP?

"I am strong. I am invincible. I am woman." — Helen Reddy

This book is for you if you are:

- Looking for a new job, either in or out of your current organization.
- Up-to-speed or coming up-to-speed with current practices on how to get a job in the industry you want.
- Generally clear about what you want to do.
- Feeling disconnected from your work and /or the mission of your organization.
- Committed to a balanced approach, taking both actions on the physical level as well as the spiritual level to find fulfilling work.
- Seeking guidance about how to infuse a new approach into your job hunt so that your work is rewarding, at both a spiritual as well as a physical level.

This book should not be your singular reference on how to get a great new job. There are other writers and experts who have excellent advice and current tips on how to win in the job hunt and career world. Instead, this book serves a unique and important purpose. This book will give you a new and different way to approach your job hunt from a more spiritual perspective. In the final pages of this book, I have included a few sources that describe solid tips on how to find a job at the physical level. By blending my approach with the rational current methods for job hunters, you will find a job that is spiritually fulfilling.

INVEST IN YOURSELF IN A NEW WAY

"Opportunity is missed by most people because it is dressed in overalls and looks like work." — Thomas Edison

My approach is not more work than a traditional job hunt. It is just different. Instead of putting all your energy into the physical steps to find a job, you will be shifting some of that time and energy into a different approach — an approach that will help you to clear out spiritual baggage and shine the light on a path to get to rewarding work.

Work is a spiritual endeavor. The time has come to approach getting a new job with respect for the spiritual side of life. In this way, your next job will appear like the most natural, logical step ever, and bring you joy along with it.

Can you do this? Absolutely. It will take work and commitment. It will take effort. It will take some soul searching and recognizing things about yourself that you both love and hate. The outcomes are worth it and your growth and spiritual life belong in your work life if you want to thrive and find real meaning in what you do.

THE MIND AND
COGNITIVE BIASES

THE MIND, COGNITIVE BIASES, AND INTUITION

I like to know what I'm doing. When I'm making a new dish, driving to a new destination, or meeting new people, I do my best to study-up and learn enough about my task to know, at least a little, about what I am trying to do.

So that you can be prepared to jump into the hunt well-informed, this chapter describes several key ideas which are foundational to the book and to the process of manifesting a new job. Here is what's included in this chapter:

- A discussion about the conscious, subconscious, and super-conscious mind.
- Cognitive biases and why they are important so you can be more aware of problems caused by this kind of thinking shortcut.
- Intuition and why many people are apprehensive to lean into it.

My hope is that after this chapter you will have a deeper appreciation for important aspects of the mind as it pertains to finding your dream job so that as you meet them in later chapters you are primed for them.

Conscious, Subconscious and Superconscious

"It is only with the heart that one can see rightly;
what is essential is invisible to the eye."
— Antoine de St-Exupery

If you have ever learned to drive a car, you know there are many things you need to know. There are the rules of the road, the vehicle itself and how it works, and finally, how you apply the knowledge to driving it. Learning to drive a car starts with a mental exercise of learning the parts, and then moves into a physical exercise on how to push the pedals and turn the wheel. There's a lot to keep track of when you begin driving. Every action requires conscious thought. You must watch the road carefully for other drivers and pedestrians. Driving takes a lot of energy to focus and execute.

Over time, driving gets easier. Practice helps. Your body gets more used to the actions you need to take, and your attention grows more attuned to the world around you. Finally it becomes an unconscious skill you have internalized.

Learning how to use the mind to manifest a job is like driving. First you need to learn some basics about how the mind works. Next, you will find that practicing makes it easier. The activities in this book will help with the practicing. Eventually you will be in the flow, just like driving a car.

The Mind

"Who am I? Not the body, because it is decaying; not the mind, because
the brain will decay with the body; not the personality, nor the emotions,
for these also will vanish with death."
— Ramana Maharshi

What is the mind? The mind exists inside and outside of your physical body. Often we equate the brain with the mind, because the brain is where most of our neurons live, but the fact is *the brain is not your mind* but a part of it. Did you know you have neurons in your heart (try thinking with your heart once in a while)?

Since the beginning of time, humans have been interested in the mind. What does the mind consist of? Clearly the brain supports the mind, but the mind is more than the brain. We have neurons in our heart. We say we have a "gut feeling" to describe an intuitive feeling. My study has led me to split the mind into three parts, the conscious, the subconscious and the superconscious. This is an upgrade to Sigmund Freud's three levels of the mind, differing slightly. Freud claimed there were three levels of the mind: the preconscious, the conscious, and the unconscious. Freud's unconscious is synonymous with my term "subconscious." The superconscious is my addition that lives outside of our individual selves and is extremely important.

The conscious mind is where we spend most of our waking time. It is that soundtrack in your head that is running constantly. Conscious thoughts might include what you think of your dinner meal, your friend's new shirt or whether you should go out next Friday night. Most of us spend so much time in our conscious mind that we often don't even think about the other levels of the mind.

The subconscious mind is the second level of the mind. We all know about the second level of the mind and it is easy to see evidence for it, but we often neglect it all the same. It is, in many ways, running the physical show. Breathing, digesting, and sweating are three functions that are maintained by the subconscious mind. Isn't it nice you don't have to rely on your conscious mind to keep your heart beating?

Your subconscious mind functions like a recorder taking in information all the time and storing it. It also makes our memories from those recordings. It stores memories as connections, often simplifying ideas as images or symbols. Embedded in your subconscious mind are programs, which are like little patterns you have adopted over time. Perhaps you have a habit of wiping your face with your napkin after a meal. This is something you don't think about consciously, you just do it. This would be a habit, a program, embedded in the subconscious mind.

One of the major reasons driving gets easier as we do more of it is thanks to the subconscious. When you first learn to drive, you must do so using your conscious mind to remember everything you learned and to direct your body to take the correct action. With practice, you rely on your subconscious to help with the driving. This is particularly helpful because our subconscious has a faster reaction time than our conscious mind does. Daniel Kahneman discusses this in depth in his book *Thinking Fast and Slow*. If you are an experienced driver, you are using both your conscious and subconscious mind to drive.

The third level of the mind is the superconscious. It's harder to recognize the superconscious because, unlike the conscious mind and the subconscious mind, it lives outside of our physical plane of existence. Remember though, there are plenty of things we know exist even though they lack a physical dimension — including love, courage and faith.

The superconscious is where we are in spirit. It is where the soul lives. While it doesn't have a physical presence, the superconscious is accessible through the subconscious. *The subconscious is the gateway to the superconscious.* To integrate our whole selves, including who we are in spirit, we must go *through* the subconscious to the superconscious state.

To understand this state, it is important to understand a little more about the state we are in when we access it. Our brain emits electromagnetic frequencies of different wavelengths depending on our state of mind. In our normal conscious state, the brain emits wavelengths of 13 to 30 Hz, a level called beta. When we are in a state of meditation or hypnosis, the brain emits wavelengths of 8 to 13 Hz, in the level called alpha. Many of the activities in this book call for an alpha level reflection. Spending time in an alpha state, giving attention to the subconscious and superconscious, and recognizing there is more to life than what we see and experience on the physical planes are all ways of opening up to spirit.

The reason many of the activities in this book call for an alpha level reflection is that we want to go beyond the level of our conscious mind into the subconscious mind to review and explore. While we can be tricked into thinking that the conscious mind is all that is, and all that is important, often there is additional wisdom available to us beyond the conscious level that should not be ignored. If you want to bring your "A" game to the job hunt, bring your subconscious! Your subconscious is the seat of your memories, habits, dreams, and inspiration and it only makes sense to include it as a key player in your job hunt.

Understanding the levels of the mind at a mental level is the first step. Driving a car gets easier as you integrate your subconscious mind. Likewise, manifesting a job gets easier as you integrate your subconscious mind. Just as when you learn to drive you must practice driving to develop the skill, practicing using your subconscious mind is part of receiving a job. For this reason, this book contains many activities that will help you practice and develop your skill at accessing and integrating your subconscious and superconscious into your job hunt.

COGNITIVE BIASES AND MANIFESTING A NEW JOB

"Life consists of what a person is thinking about all day."
— Ralph Waldo Emerson

As a student of the mind, I believe a book about the powers of the mind would be incomplete without reference to cognitive biases. A cognitive bias is a systematic error in rational thinking that occurs when people are processing and interpreting information that affects decisions and judgments. Cognitive biases can be related to memory or to attention. Cognitive biases have been shown to influence our social behavior, emotions, motivations, and decision-making.

Cognitive biases generally come from the subconscious level of the mind. When we succumb to a cognitive bias, it is generally because our brain is trying to use a shortcut to get to an answer based on associative thinking. Over thousands of generations, the human mind has evolved to favor using shortcuts — they are fast and often right.

It is important to have a basic understanding of what cognitive biases are, what characterizes some of the most common cognitive biases, and how they could influence your job hunt so that you can be aware of instances when you might be taking shortcuts that aren't helpful.

Daniel Kahneman is widely considered the father of the idea of cognitive bias. *Thinking Fast and Slow* is a comprehensive book about many cognitive biases that have been shown to exist in global populations. Scientists have identified at least 50 cognitive biases. Below I describe four common cognitive biases with examples that illustrate how these thinking patterns could impact your job hunt.

Anchoring bias. Anchoring bias is the tendency to rely too much on the first information you learn. For example, if you are interviewing for a new job, and a hiring manager tells you that their organization pays $150,000 in salary for this job, anchoring bias could make you think that $150,000 is the going rate. In reality, $150,000 could be at the extreme low end of the appropriate salary or the extreme high end. Anchoring bias can lead one to make poor decisions if the first information is not accurate.

Confirmation bias. Confirmation bias is sticking with information that conforms to your beliefs. For example, if you've heard negative things about the boss at a company before you even meet her, you might not be objective when you meet her, because confirmation bias would make you notice negative things about her first.

Availability bias. Availability bias is when you weigh information that you have heard recently too much because the information is highly "available" in your mind. For example, if you have recently had a series of uncomfortable interviews that didn't go well, you are more likely to believe that an upcoming interview will be uncomfortable because the interviews in recent memory have tainted your perspective. This could negatively impact your ability to do your best at your next interview.

Negativity bias. Negativity bias is when things of a more negative nature, such as negative thoughts, emotions and traumatic events, have a greater influence on your psychological state and thinking process than neutral or positive things. For example, if you have been sending out many resumés and not getting any attention, negativity bias could make you think that you will *never* get any attention when sending out future resumés.

Cognitive biases are like little traps we can fall in. These traps can make us draw irrational conclusions in our conscious thinking and spend time in thought patterns that are not constructive.

In tapping into our deeper self, it is helpful to have a basic understanding of cognitive biases and how they can steer us in the wrong direction. Pay attention to your thought patterns. Just like with your driving, if you know that there may be traffic ahead, or a construction zone, you can plan for it and not get stuck. In the words of the Grail Knight from Indiana Jones, "Choose wisely".

THE IMPORTANCE OF INTUITION

"Have the courage to follow your heart and intuition. They somehow already know what you truly want to become. Everything else is secondary."
— Steve Jobs

As described in the Introduction, the American workplace has become almost synonymous with reason, definitions, and measurement. If you can't see it or touch it or show how it is helping, it must not even exist. In my experience, this makes most organizations anti-intuition.

I believe the reason organizations today dislike the idea of intuition is because they are uncomfortable recognizing the territory of the subconscious and superconscious mind. Organizations prefer to live in a strictly conscious place, with facts and figures, charts and memos that all speak as clearly as possible to what is on the surface and easy to talk about. When organizations think and communicate at the conscious level, it makes their messages and relationships easy for others to understand because everything is at the same conscious, or surface level.

I, on the other hand, am a firm believer in intuition, and I believe that increasing your trust in your intuition will help to put your energies in productive directions. If you are unhappy in your work or seeking a new job, your intuition should be the most, or one of the most, important guides to finding work you love. If you are happy in your work, deepening your trust in your intuition can make you more productive and feel authentic in the work you do.

What is intuition? Simply put, it is what one feels to be true in the absence of conscious reasoning. Intuition is when you know something is true, but you don't know why. Intuition is when we receive a "knowing" from our subconscious or superconscious.

Sometimes intuition can be dead on right and sometimes it's not. Clearly, as I illustrated in the examples of cognitive bias, thinking that comes from our subconscious can be flawed and even lead us astray. It is vital to recognize that not all thoughts from our subconscious are necessarily correct. The subconscious has patterns and programs of thinking, and if those patterns or programs produce the wrong answer, your intuition will be wrong.

However, many people undervalue what intelligence we *can* receive from our subconscious and superconscious. Because our internal thoughts are sometimes wrong does not negate the fact they are often right. What I have found is that the subconscious has an enormous amount of knowledge about what companies and jobs are a good match. The subconscious is able to weave together memories, experience, and opportunities in ways that the conscious mind cannot. The subconscious and sometimes the superconscious can see where and how there could be a match between a company and a candidate in ways that a resumé cannot.

Of all the mistakes I have made job hunting, the one I have made the most often is pursuing jobs that my subconscious mind warned me about. I have wasted a great deal of time preparing resumés, cover letters, making phone calls and interviewing for jobs that my subconscious doubted.

One of my strengths for the many challenges I have faced in my life is a rather extreme degree of optimism. I have a way of absorbing bad news and turning it around the next day into a perspective of hope and opportunity that is rather extraordinary. For the most part, my talent in optimism has served me very well, helping me get through the losses of the loves in my life, job losses, and parenting. However, my high level of optimism has sometimes been detrimental to my job hunt, particularly when I let my optimism override direction coming from my subconscious.

Here is an example of one occasion when I failed to listen to my subconscious and made an unfortunate choice. A few years ago, after several months of looking for a new position, I came across a posting for a small consulting company I had never heard of. I checked Linkedin and no one in my network seemed to be connected to this company. The company appeared to be privately held and small, but was working for some large and impressive clients. The website looked professional and the company was located driving distance from my home. Because I had experience that was relevant to the job and because I did a great job of ensuring my resumé spoke very specifically to their needs, they called me in for an interview.

When I arrived, I could see that this company was like no other I had ever interviewed at before. I had some trouble finding the office. The directory by the elevator indicated the offices were in the "Penthouse". I took the elevator to the top floor, but the offices were not there. I needed to climb an additional flight of stairs to reach what I would have called the roof, where the offices were situated. I have always been a strong advocate for access for the disabled, and it troubled me to be interviewing in an office that was not wheelchair accessible.

When I found the offices, there were three rooms. The rooms were small. Two of the rooms had three or four Ikea student desks crammed into them, and there were about six people working at those desks. Everyone was wearing headphones in an attempt to feel more independent. The receptionist had blue hair and treated me with disdain. The third room served as the CEO's office. My interview was with her in her office.

The interview went fine, although I felt a little disrespected by the tone of the CEO. She seemed to understand how my background prepared me for this job, but she seemed a little skeptical instead of being genuinely supportive. Regardless, she needed experience and talent and she made me an offer.

My intuition was speaking to me about this job and it was aware there was a mismatch. In my desire to start a job I didn't listen. Deep in my heart, I knew this was a poor fit. I took the job regardless of my inner knowing that this was a step in the wrong direction.

Although my boss was very accomplished, she wasn't a good fit for someone with my background. My largest client was extremely difficult to please, hard to understand, and on occasion irrational, unprofessional, and just plain rude. I did have a great team and I did learn a lot. However, the biggest lesson I learned from this negative experience was to trust my intuition. If the job feels wrong, there's a very good chance it is.

DELAYING INTUITION

"The only real valuable thing is intuition." — Albert Einstein

While your intuition is a critical tool in your ability to steer and make decisions, there is good evidence that it works best when combined with solid analysis. Daniel Kahneman cites research he led over 50 years ago for the Israeli army as an example of how to integrate intuition into decision-making.

As a young university graduate in Psychology, Kahneman was assigned by the army in 1955 to define a method for selecting army personnel for combat. He composed a set of interview questions that assessed six different traits relevant to combat, such as responsibility and sociability. The interviewers scored participants on these traits and an algorithm predicted each soldier's combat readiness.

The interviewers didn't like Kahneman's new process. Prior to his arrival, the interviewers assessed the soldiers' readiness using their own questions and process. When Kahneman's process started, their individual input ended.

To appease the interviewers, Kahneman agreed to add to his interview process a step after the questions. The interviewer was asked to close his eyes and to imagine the soldier in combat and score them intuitively on a scale of 1 – 10. Kahneman was genuinely surprised to discover that the best predictor of combat readiness was a combination of the algorithms and the interviewer's intuitive score.

"Delay intuition," is Kahneman's advice. By first following an analytic framework, the structured questions and the algorithm, and *then* adding the interviewer's intuitive sense, the process worked best. For this reason, it's important to combine both your conscious, rational, analytic thinking with your subconscious wisdom when evaluating opportunities and taking action.

Because I am a strong advocate of intuition, I view this as sound advice. When looking for a job, there are many, many factors to consider: 1) Can I make a success out of this? 2) Are the hours reasonable? 3) Is the commute ok? It is important to know what you are looking for — and what is a must-have versus a nice-to-have. It is necessary to learn as much as possible about the opportunity, and then to bounce that up against your personal needs and desires to see if there is a match. Then listen to your intuition.

The takeaway is this: *be sure to include your intuition*. Your intuition is where you add in the subconscious and superconscious levels and upgrade your results.

Including your intuition is not just a step to use in your final decision-making about accepting a job, but also a key tool to use all through the job hunt, including where you apply, how and when to follow-up, and what to say. The activities will help illustrate many ways to use your intuition.

THE METHOD

The Manifestation Wheel

"You create your thoughts, your thoughts create your intentions, and your intentions create your reality." — Wayne Dyer

Many books have been written on how to use the Manifestation Wheel to attract money, wonderful relationships, and real estate. This book applies it to a new category: work.

While a big part of manifesting your dream job comes from your mind, mind work alone is unlikely to bring you success. For that reason, I have created easy, fun activities to help you focus your energy and send and receive messages from the universe to guide you in your quest. The activities are all about honing in on energy and sending it in positive directions to manifest your dream job.

In case you're worried about using the Manifestation Wheel to get a job, don't be! It is a sound method that works. The Manifestation Wheel has four spokes: Release, Create, Thank and Receive. In the following section we will discuss the four spokes of the wheel quickly to give you an understanding of how they work together. Following that, we will talk about how to work on them. In the chapters that follow we will go into greater detail on each of the spokes and the activities you can do for each.

RELEASE

"If you are to advance, all fixed ideas must go." — Joseph Campbell

In 2005, my life was not going so well. While I was blessed with a loving husband who had received a life-saving lung transplant, a precious toddler and a seventeen year old stepson, my husband Bruce had been unable to find reliable paid work for years. Bruce had dropped out of the tech world when his lungs were failing, and had not managed to get back into tech after his surgery. My stepson was struggling with drug and alcohol problems. Bruce was depressed and I was overburdened trying to provide for a family of four in the Bay Area. It seemed like there was no possible re-mix of the elements of our lives that would bring us stability and lasting happiness.

After months of discussion, Bruce and I opted to make a bold move. Instead of trying to fix our situation in California, we opted to jump ship. Because we had both lived in Texas before and the cost of living in Texas was lower than California, we opted to return to Texas. We sold our second car, ditched unwanted furniture, and packed a truck. We leased out our house in California. I gave notice at my job in San Francisco and left for Texas without a job. We let our California life go, in faith a better one was waiting for us in Texas.

We arrived in Texas and started putting together a simple life and quickly reaching out to potential employers. I found a job with an agency where several former colleagues worked within two months. Bruce found a good job in the tech industry through his Texan connections. My stepson got his life back on track for a time, although his addiction problems resurfaced a few months later. My toddler was a happy kid, no matter where he was.

Releasing can be hard. Even if what you need to release is not as dramatic as moving to another state, it can be hard. Often, it is important to consider what releasing work you do need to do to make the change you want to make.

Release must come first. Everyone, besides maybe a saint, is carrying around something that needs to be released. For most of us, our negative cognitive biases are the very first things we might want to work on. We know they are part of being human, and that they were created to help us, but for our job search, they may get in the way. Here is one example of how a cognitive bias could have factored into my thinking: if I had allowed myself to get caught up in thinking that our fate would be the same in Texas as California, I would not have left California and found new work.

Along with cognitive biases, we all also have emotional baggage. Some have more and some have less, but, let's be honest, we all have some.

A common question that comes up here is, "Sure, I have emotional baggage I carry around, but most of it is about my [topic x, e.g. my mother, my upbringing, my husband], not about work or my job. Since it's not about my work or my job, it must be irrelevant."

Not so! You are unconsciously applying a very this-leads-to-that mentality to the world of spirit. While it's perfectly fine to observe that "adding milk to my cereal makes it taste good," which is like a (milk) + b (cereal) leads to = c (tastes good), the world of spirit is much more complicated. In the world of spirit, connections come from and go to all kinds of places. The world of spirit is more like a map of the stars than a table of math problems. Assuming that if you have no emotional baggage you see connected to work means you have nothing to release is false thinking.

Release includes the steps of acceptance of forgiveness. You might have emotional baggage you need to get rid of that doesn't include forgiveness. Forgiveness is an integral part of the process and necessary to explore as part of spiritually attracting a new job.

More specific activities will follow in chapter five.

CREATE

"If you want to find the secrets of the universe, think in terms of energy, frequency and vibration." — Nikola Tesla

The step of Create follows release. Create is without a doubt my favorite step. Creating is the process of imagining your new job.

Just like it takes paint, paintbrushes, and paper to create a painting, it takes resources to create a new job. Some of these resources are things you can touch or name, and some of them are ideas or images wholly contained in the mind's eye.

On the physical plane, you may need training to get a new job. You may need to know people, or need contacts or references. You may need experience that evidences how you can provide value to a new organization. Taking a spiritual approach to your job hunt does not overcome the need to meet the criteria potential colleagues and employers expect on the physical plane.

Sometimes it is easy to create a wonderful job. In 1999, the first time I lived in Texas, I was working for a great employer in Texas as a Technology Consultant. My job was to serve as a bridge between the marketing and advertising managers and the technology team to design and deploy database marketing programs for our clients. I loved the company, and I liked the work. I just didn't like Texas.

The dot com bubble was expanding, and most of its activity was in California. I wanted to return to the Bay Area to be near my family and friends, to be closer to the action in the dot com world, and to enjoy the outstanding weather and wonderful nature that California has to offer.

I'm a very honest and open person, and it was no secret that I was missing home. My employer valued my work and wanted to retain me. We came to an excellent arrangement. My company changed my job to be an Account Manager, directly interfacing with clients. While I was no longer the primary technical advisor, I was happy to have a very important role in the business. My company put me in charge of a client in Southern California, and I did an excellent job of serving and growing that business from a home office in the Bay Area. The right job was created just for me.

The spiritual side of looking for a job is where mental imagery comes into play. This is the step where you imagine what your desk or workspace might look like. It is the step where you imagine the kinds of projects you will work on, and the feeling of working on those projects. The Create step is extremely important to the Manifestation Wheel, because without it, the Universe doesn't know what you desire.

More specific activities will follow in chapter seven.

Thank

"Gratitude turns what we have into enough." — Anonymous

In our fast-paced society, it's very easy to overlook the importance of making time for thankfulness. As considerable recent research has come to show, gratitude is practically a miracle cure for all kinds of things. We know now what our grandmothers told us when we were young, that giving thanks is good for us.

In the process of looking for a new job, gratitude is a critical step to aligning our spirit with our search and our success.

While job hunting I often recall great people I have worked with and my gratitude towards them.

I moved to Texas in 1997 after finishing graduate school in Seattle. My boss, the VP of Technology, was a beautiful lady named Debbie. Debbie and I liked each other very much and had an excellent professional and personal relationship.

Unfortunately, I was rather lonely in Texas. I knew almost no one in the area, and moving for a job in your late twenties to another state is hard on the social life. For my birthday, Debbie gave me a gift that is still giving over twenty years later.

Debbie introduced me to Karen. Karen was a Dallas-based world-renowned intuitive and teacher. Karen's understanding of the heart and the spirit side was deeper and truer than anyone I have ever met. Karen was a teacher and a therapist to me off and on for decades. Many of my viewpoints come directly or indirectly from her. Sadly, Karen passed in 2021 before I had a chance to tell her I was writing this book.

The connections and gratitude extend further. It is thanks to Karen and Debbie that I found my publisher and editor for this book. One small gift of a session in 1998 has led to decades of love and support, and even the people I needed for this book. I am so thankful.

Like Create, the Thank step doesn't have to be exclusively connected to the idea of getting a job. The Universe sees everything as connected, so you can be thankful for things that you might not view as related to your job hunt and still be moving to manifest your job. It is legitimate to be thankful for chocolate chip cookies, beautiful sunsets and small acts of kindness. Even those moments of gratitude are part of doing the spiritual work necessary for your job hunt.

More specific activities will follow in chapter nine.

RECEIVE

"And I know when I'm on track — that is, when everything is in a harmonious relationship to what I regard as the best I've got in me."
— Joseph Campbell

The fourth spoke of the Manifestation Wheel is Receive. Receiving requires skill and practice. I know some people who are excellent at receiving, and I know other people who are terrible at receiving. My story about receiving is how I found my house.

I had always dreamed of having a home near downtown with my loving family living in it. On a hot day in June 1999, I was looking for a place to live the old-fashioned way — by driving around interesting neighborhoods and looking for For Rent signs. I was driving a red convertible VW Rabbit with the top down. My cute, blonde girlfriend and I pulled over to stop for a cold drink. She stood on the sidewalk while I put up the top on the car since we would be parked for a few minutes.

"What kind of a car you girls' got there?" said an old man waddling down the sidewalk. This fellow looked to be over eighty years old.

"A convertible!" said my girlfriend, stating the obvious.

"It's a Rabbit," I said, trying to be a little more specific, and kind of wondering about this old guy, and wondering if my friend could sound any less blonde.

"What are you up to today?" said the old man.

"We are looking for a house for my friend to rent," said my girlfriend. I was a little concerned about her friendliness and openness with this unknown old guy on the sidewalk, but there was no going back.

"Really?" said the old man. "My house is for rent. It's a couple of blocks from here. My wife is home watching the tennis match today. We are moving to live near our son who is a pastor at a congregation up the coast. We are going to rent out the house and maybe sell it in the future if we like living near our son."

My girlfriend and I looked at each other. This wasn't how we imagined finding me a place to live. We got the address from the old man and went to get our drinks.

Within a month, I had moved into that house. Three months later, my fiancé Bruce moved in. Within three years, we got married, purchased the house, had a baby, and moved in my stepson. The house, which came to me via a chance conversation on the sidewalk was my beautiful home for over twenty years.

Of course, not everyone will find a house by running into an old man who comes up with one, but sometimes things do arrive serendipitously. It is important to keep an open mind.

It is possible to be a poor receiver. One way to be a poor receiver is simply not noticing that someone is trying to give you something. If you can't recognize that you've been given a chance for an introduction, an invitation for dinner, or a smile from a stranger, you might have a problem with receiving.

Another way you might be poor at receiving is if you are averse to asking for anything. If you have done the work of the Manifestation Wheel, and truly done the activities at each step, you won't have this problem because you will have asked for something in the Create step. Skipping the Create step can lead to a problem in receiving.

The third way you may be a poor receiver is to be a poor giver. The Universe wants to find balance in all things, and that includes the back and forth of giving and receiving. Those who give, receive.

More specific activities will follow in chapter eleven.

EXTERNAL WORK

"Change your thoughts and you will change your world."
— Norman Vincent Peale

The Manifestation Wheel takes action on both a physical and spiritual level to produce results. As you study, you must also work on the physical level to make your job arrive.

Updating your LinkedIn page, sending out resumés, calling former employers, or taking classes to update your skills may all be required to win a new job. *It is imperative you make the necessary time for those activities.* The Universe is listening to your spiritual work as you pursue the new job. The Universe is also listening to see if your actions on the physical plane show that you want a job. Skip the physical work and the Universe will not think you are serious in your request.

Just as I was a beneficiary of the rise of the dot com era, I was collateral damage in the dot bomb wave. Like so many others, I spent months out of work in 2000. There were no jobs to be found.

Finally, in late 2000, I found out there may be an opening in San Francisco at an advertising agency. I was particularly interested in this opportunity for several reasons: 1) I had worked for a sister agency in Texas and some of my benefits would transfer, 2) The agency was working on a local account in the same industry as I had worked on before, and 3) I would be working part time in an office in San

Francisco and part time at the client's offices in the East Bay, which sounded fun and super convenient. It looked like a great fit. And yet, there were so many people out of work. How would I stand out?

I took a multi-tiered approach. Applying through the standard channels was unlikely to be loud enough to get the attention I needed. I wanted to make sure the hiring manager heard about my candidacy from many directions. I figured if he heard about me from multiple sources, he would think it was important to talk to me, and I knew that if I got the interview, I would almost certainly get the job, despite stiff competition.

I reached out to Human Resources (HR) at the San Francisco agency and told them about my excellent qualifications. I had someone from HR at the sister agency call San Francisco and assure them I was a strong candidate. Someone I met through a friend was a vendor to the San Francisco agency, and I had her call the hiring manager and tell him he should call me. It took every lever I could pull, but I did get his attention, the interview, and the job. It is critical to do the physical work necessary to get your dream job.

As you begin using a spiritual approach to your job hunt you will find that you have a better idea of what actions on the physical front are most likely to bear fruit. It is a natural part of the process that by spending more time and energy on the spiritual side of the job hunt than you may have in the past, you will find it easier to recognize what actions on the physical front are worthwhile.

Several of the activities in the following four chapters focus on this. For example, doing the activities may bring on a dream which includes a former colleague you haven't talked to lately, and a phone call to that former colleague leads to an interview. Be open to what comes.

One of the activities I will teach you involves using your intuition to help you prioritize which opportunities to focus on. I have used this technique many times over my various job hunts. By relaxing my mind to a deep level, and using graphical representations of my opportunities, I have been able to hear my inner guidance in ways that I couldn't before. This activity helped me to choose which opportunities to actively pursue, and which opportunities to skip. As a result, I pursued the better jobs that were a possible match for me and didn't waste my time and energy on opportunities that were not a fit. This activity is included in the chapter on Creating.

INTERNAL WORK

"Healing doesn't mean the damage never existed. It means the damage no longer controls our life." — Akshay Dubey

For people who are attached to rational processes where it is clear that a leads to b leads to c, approaching a job hunt from this perspective may feel risky or scary. That is understandable. From the time we are young, most of us have been taught to believe what we can physically see. If you haven't used a spiritual perspective in your job hunt before, I'm asking you to take a leap of faith and try it.

Manifesting your new job may feel difficult at first, but it does get easier with time and practice. Like many things, the more you do it, the more enjoyable it is and the more you will trust the process.

For the rest of this chapter, we will talk about what that internal work looks like. In the chapters that follow I will lead you through activities to do this work. It's okay if these steps are new to you; it's why you picked up this book in the first place. And it's also okay if you find that the internal and external work are intertwined. In fact, you will have a lot of feelings and experiences as you move into this internal work. After over 18 personal job hunts and watching the progress of my clients, I can tell you all of them are probably normal and common.

Doing the Activities

"A year from now you will wish you had started today." — Karen Lamb

Unlike other activities you may have worked through for your job hunt, the activities in this book have been constructed to deepen your connection to spirit and your subconscious. It may take some practice understanding how to do these activities so that they will have their intended impact.

When working on these activities, you want to submerge yourself at a level that goes beyond your conscious, rational mind. You want to tap into the power of your subconscious and spirit. These activities, done thoroughly, will likely bring up your emotions. You may experience joy at surfacing a positive memory from the past, or anger with yourself for making a compromise you later regretted. Surfacing these emotions is a critical part of this work. Emotions are spiritual fuel — they propel change, self-realization, and growth. If you are honestly desiring a change in your work, experiencing emotions will help you attain it.

It's worth mentioning again; taking a spiritual approach to getting a job is an adjunct strategy. The activities in this book will not replace all the other things you will have to do on a conscious physical plane to get a job. If your resumé needs work, if your interviewing skills are weak, if you need certificates or training for a job, you must do those things. Frequently though, even those activities are easier to see and accomplish when worked on in parallel with the spiritual approach.

There are three types of activities in this book. This section provides guidance about how to do the activities.

- Writing
- Art
- Alpha Level Exploration (Self-hypnosis or Meditation)

WRITING

"I can shake off everything as I write.
My sorrows disappear, my courage is reborn." — Anne Frank

Many of the activities in this book call for writing. Writing is an outstanding way of bringing up our truth and allowing us to both think and reflect as we go.

Writing by hand in a journal is my recommended means of doing these activities, because studies have shown that the process of physically writing makes a more indelible imprint on the brain than writing on a computer or digital device. Still, what's important is getting the writing done, and if doing it on the computer makes it easier to do and keep up, that's just fine.

Many of the writing activities also call for a meditation or self-hypnosis session. This is further discussed in the self-hypnosis section below.

ART

"Art must be an expression of love, or it is nothing." — Marc Chagall

Because our minds process ideas in images, it is very helpful to make images as a means of speaking to and hearing from the mind. A lot of businesspeople can be overly self-critical when it comes to self-made art. However, the only person who will see the artwork you produce from these activities is you, unless you choose to share it.

While a number two pencil and printer paper will do in a pinch, consider upgrading to colored pencils or crayons and potentially oversized paper, like from a conference room easel. Our lives on earth are meant to be rich, full lives, filled with color and textures and shadows. Live it up a little and make the imagery you use to speak with your mind colorful and big!

I do recommend you make one of the art activities on the computer. I have found this activity particularly helpful because it taps into other invisible spiritual connections. Another art activity includes making a collage which is best made physically. For this activity, you can use magazines for pictures or you can search for images on the internet, print them, and stick them to your board. I recommend a piece of cardboard or foam board at least 14 x 20 for this Receive activity.

As with the writing activities, the art activities are step one; a reflection step typically follows. These activities all start by opening the door to the subconscious via the conscious mind, followed by an exploration of the subconscious mind, where spirit and mind exist.

EXPLORING YOUR SUBCONSCIOUS: THE ALPHA LEVEL

"Quiet the mind and the soul will speak." — Ma Jaya Sati Bhagati

Several of the activities in this book start with the subconscious and many of them include a second step where you will access your subconscious. The technique I prefer is self-hypnosis. Self-hypnosis is an excellent technique, especially for business-minded people to access the subconscious.

If, however, you are practiced at an alternative means of processing at the subconscious level, like mindfulness meditation, then use your own technique. What is important is that you access these topics at the subconscious level, where the brain is in the relaxed state called alpha.

Self-hypnosis is a process of relaxing so much that you shift from your awake state, where your brain is producing brain waves in the beta brainwave spectrum, to a lower frequency wave called alpha. This is accomplished by becoming so relaxed that your mind becomes hyperfocused and your complete attention is given over to one thing. Have you ever been so engrossed in a movie that you have forgotten yourself? Or driven somewhere on the highway and forgot the details of how you got from your starting point to your destination? These are both occasions when your mind shifts, and you change your brainwave pattern. The same thing happens just before you fall asleep and just as you wake up.

To experience the state of self-hypnosis, find yourself a very comfortable chair and make sure you won't be disturbed. A recliner works well, but you can also do this in your desk chair or even seated on the floor. I don't recommend doing this in your bed if you have another comfortable alternative, because being in bed may make you think of sleep and you are not trying to sleep. Many people find music relaxing and you may choose to play some soft music while you do your activities. Breathe deeply and close your eyes. Imagine a light shining on the top of your head and moving down slowly across every muscle of your body, all the way to your fingers and toes. Take at least five minutes, or even ten, to get more and more relaxed. This is the point where you will start each self-hypnosis activity.

If you're still unsure if you are doing it right, please see my website at www.michellewalters.net where you can download a hypnosis recording and learn more about the practice of hypnosis.

In the next chapters we will go into deeper exploration of the four spokes and then the activities that accompany your journey through them.

RELEASE

RELEASE

"Life is full and overflowing with the new. But it is necessary to empty out the old to make room for the new to enter." — Eileen Caddy

It might sound backwards, but the first step in getting a job is actually about letting go. Just like you probably don't have room for a new sofa unless you get rid of the one you've got, you have to release energy to bring in something new. If you are working and seeking a new job, it isn't necessary to quit your job to find another, but you need to find some ways to release energy. Releasing is part of setting the energy of the Universe in motion and you need to start there. Look out your window. What season is it? If it's spring, then spring arrived when winter let go. If it's fall, fall came after summer ended. With each turn of the seasons, the last season had to happen and then let go in order to make room for the next one. Changes, like seasons, are based on patterns. Develop, then release, then develop again. This is the natural way.

We grow up observing the world with a Newtonian view, focusing on the matter before our eyes, but we know that is an incomplete picture. Einstein advanced science with his famous equation, $E = mc^2$. Matter is simply the case when light is frozen. We are constantly surrounded by energy; some of that energy is in a state of matter. In other words, everything is energy.

Einstein also showed us that our belief that time can be divided into the past, present and future is actually an illusion. The theory of relativity says that time is a tapestry of a four-dimensional space-time continuum that encompasses the past, present and future.

These concepts are important in manifesting your dream job because it's important to open the mind to new information and interpretations. The more you allow yourself to detach from expecting constant order and material explanation, the easier you will find it to turn the Manifestation Wheel.

Getting the energy of your job right is important because we spend something like 25 percent of our lives at work. Our work is a major way our energy, both physical and spiritual, interacts with the universe. Through our work, we exchange energy with the Universe and other earth energies, most notably, other people. We need to make that time feel good and be aligned with our spirit to get the most out of life.

Another reason people resist release is they think, "I don't have negative baggage from my work, so why do I need to do release work to get a new job?" This argument is also flawed.

Our lives have become so hectic and challenging that it's common practice to compartmentalize thoughts and experiences. Many of us manage our day by having our specific hours set aside for specific activities such as work, family, play, and church. We organize the kid's time into friend time, school time, practice time, etc. We organize restaurants into the ones we frequent versus the ones we hold for special occasions. Our money is organized into spending and saving. In our efforts to maximize our life experiences and not go insane, we put things into buckets.

Often, we are reluctant to admit that what happens in one area of our life impacts others, but if you step back, you know this is true. An hour spent with the kids is an hour you don't have to send emails.

Taking time to have a girl's weekend may mean missing an important meeting at the office. The fact is our life is one big experience and it's all related. If you think you have nothing to release because you don't see any Release issues as work issues, you are thinking too small. Everything impacts work and so you need to look deeper and wider.

The step of Release is to drop negative energy. Negative energies are the things that make you feel bad. Along with your cognitive biases, which are often negative because they are protective mechanisms, we also hold shame, guilt and fear. Everyone has these feelings. Some of us feel them multiple times every day while others feel them less often. Negative energies make us yell, cry, and sometimes make us feel like we want to hide under a rock. It is critical to let go of excessive negative energies to make space for the energy you want more of, the positive energy.

This book cannot function as a complete treatise on how to let go of all negative energy in your life. It can, however, show you or remind you how to notice negative energy and teach you ways to release it. The teachings and activities in this book will go a long way to casting away negative energy that can interfere with your job hunt. For some readers, you may need to do more releasing work than what is covered in this book. Please check the references for this chapter or work with a personal therapist if these release methods help you realize that you want or need to do more.

What will you get from completing the Release step? The biggest benefit people cite from completing their Release work is a greater sense of inner peace. Releasing feels good and accelerates the arrival of changes and positive energy. It is very difficult, even impossible, to attract good things if you are deep in negative energy.

Energy can also be stagnant and need to be released. Energy likes to be in motion, and if it is tied up too tightly, it can get in the way of the arrival of positive things and events.

For example, my husband and I had invested a great deal of energy into fixing up a lovely old house we bought. We both went through multiple periods of being unemployed, and one of the ways we passed the time waiting for the next job to come through was by painting rooms, removing old structures in the garden, replacing the sink in the bathroom, and a great number of other minor house projects. This work was productive and enjoyable for us.

Several years later, after my husband passed, I found myself between jobs again. While I loved looking around my house at the many projects and upgrades my husband and I had done together, it was very clear that his energy was all over my house and garden. I loved the sage green living rooms walls we painted together, the basement office we had both worked in, and the plants we had put in our front garden, but it was time for a change. I knew that I needed to release, and in this case, I needed to release energy related to my husband Bruce, by redoing rooms in the house and updating the garden.

I set to. I decided to work only with paint, pictures on the walls, and plants because these were all low-cost projects I could do myself. Other projects that Bruce and I had done together, like tiling in the kitchen and bathroom, I preserved. By repainting about 60 percent of the house, changing some of my wall art, and replacing a few plants outdoors, the energy of the house changed completely. Bruce's thumbprint was still on the house, but it was no longer the dominant energy. Soon after I finished the work, I found another job.

If you have recently lost a job and want to find another one, I highly recommend looking around your environment and making some changes. Our environments, meaning our home, car, and neighborhood, all have energies associated with them. It is helpful to our minds to change things when shifting from one work environment to another.

The magnitude of the work change can influence what changes you make to your environment. Not all job losses necessitate repainting 60 percent of a house. A new tablecloth, curtains, or moving furniture or artwork can go a long way. You can also shift energy by just doing things differently, like taking a different route to the grocery store. The goal is to make changes to your physical environment so that your spirit and subconscious perceive a shift. This helps to release and let in new opportunities.

Releasing is hard for most of us, and that's not a bad thing. Here's why. If you find releasing easy, it means that you don't invest a lot of energy into what you care about, so it isn't that hard to let it go. When releasing is hard, it means that there is a lot of spiritual energy tied up in what you are letting go. This indicates that you know how to care about things, you know how to create spiritual energy, and you have big, or at least good-sized, emotions. Emotions are fuel for change. So, if releasing is hard, think of it as a good thing. It means you know how to make strong attachments. You can use that power to make more of the attachments, like a job, you want in the future.

RELEASING AND FORGIVENESS

"When you hold resentment toward another, you are bound to that person or condition by an emotional link that is stronger than steel. Forgiveness is the only way to dissolve that link and get free."
— Catherine Ponder

Releasing and forgiveness are not the same thing, but they are related. Releasing is the more general term. Releasing is to let go of built up spiritual energy. Forgiveness is also a letting go of spiritual energy, but in the case of forgiveness, there is an additional aspect — that you feel wronged.

I find it easier to think first about releasing, and then when that well has dried up, to turn my attention to forgiveness. Working through it this way allows for a more cyclic and complete process, where I can release, forgive, and then do more releasing and forgiving if necessary.

Forgiving is the special condition of releasing where you feel wronged or slighted in some way. Maybe you need to forgive your spouse for taking a job that has him working more hours than you expected. Maybe you need to forgive your boss for putting too much on your plate because too much was put on her plate. Maybe you need to forgive your doctor for running late and then making you late.

We all have things that come up, nearly every day, where there is space for forgiveness. It's fine and natural to feel slighted or wronged when things happen. Noticing that feeling is the first step. The goal is not to never feel bad when things happen, the goal is to learn to let them go through forgiving.

For some people, forgiveness comes quite naturally. Often, the people who can forgive and move on had good models of forgiveness in their childhood and developed patterns early in life of feeling wronged and then forgiving.

If forgiveness doesn't come easily to you now, the good news is you can practice and get better. It is important to be able to forgive because if you hold back on forgiving, you are retaining unnecessary negative energy.

And, as much as forgiveness does benefit the person we forgive, that is not the only positive impact. It took me a very long time to realize that the major beneficiary of forgiveness was me.

I had broken up with a boyfriend, and while I was absolutely sure it was the right thing to do, it was still painful. Our relationship had become long distance and it had been sort of on-again, off-again for several months. He told me he had found someone else and while I should have realized this was to be expected, it triggered me and I became anxious and jealous. Those feelings were a reasonable reaction to the situation, but I didn't want to stay there. Next, I had a sort of epiphany! I realized I could just forgive him and let it go. A tremendous weight fell off my shoulders and I knew I could move forward with bringing new, good events into my life.

Forgiving other people takes practice. No one has mastered forgiving. We have to also learn to forgive ourselves. Forgiving ourselves can be harder even than forgiving other people. This is common among budding perfectionists and high achievers. We can feel like we didn't give a situation our all, that we are less than perfect as a result, and the only person we have to blame is ourselves.

Don't let yourself fall into this trap! We all miss deadlines, forget appointments and send emails before we've finished. You deserve your own forgiveness. Strive for doing great work, but be ready to give yourself a break when you need it. Listen to your colleagues and show respect for others. If you mess up, acknowledge it, let the forgiveness happen, and move on.

For some people forgiving can be a daily activity, and that's perfectly fine. We can't stop or change the feeling that we have been wronged or slighted. It happens naturally and so fast that it is very difficult to interrupt the thought. Notice the thought, forgive, and let it go. You don't want to hold on to negative energy any longer than absolutely necessary.

RELEASE AND HEALING

"We must be willing to get rid of the life we've planned,
so as to have the life that is waiting for us." — Joseph Campbell

Releasing is a form of healing. Many ailments are related to problems with Release. High blood pressure and clogged arteries would benefit from the release of cholesterol and increased elasticity for the arteries. Muscle pain is often caused by muscles that are stuck in a routine of clenching too tightly. Depression is an example of holding on to negative thoughts that feel impossible to let go. Frequently, releasing can bring better physical or mental well-being.

Excess stress is something many of us suffer from today. The world has become very busy. It has become normal for many of us to live in a state of chronic stress. Releasing ourselves from some of that stress by setting new boundaries, saying "no," and prioritizing self-care can be an important step to feeling better and clearing the path for more gifts from the Universe.

Releasing is choosing to not let something continue to have power over you — and if that's not possible, finding ways to change things up so that the burden feels lighter. Many years ago, my husband was hospitalized for over six months after suffering a serious infection and a stroke. I would have liked to walk away and let go of the situation, but I was committed to my marriage and responsibilities. The responsibility of taking care of my two-year-old son fell to me. Because we had no family in the area and I worked full time, this was quite a burden. I didn't have the option to stop taking care of my son during this time, but I could make changes to make the burden a little lighter.

Since I couldn't bring my toddler to the hospital, I found a woman who lived near the hospital and ran an in-home day care to take care of him a couple of nights a week for an hour so I could visit my husband. I had to release my need to do everything myself and find new ways of being and doing to meet the situation. Because of her help and flexibility, I was able to balance time with both my son and my husband during this extremely difficult time.

When a complete release isn't possible, take stock of your resources and review your options. Odds are you can find a window to open somewhere.

WHY LESS IS MORE AND MORE IS LESS

"The secret to happiness is low expectations." — Barry Schwartz

Part of releasing is coming to terms with the idea that in many cases, less is more. What do I mean by this? As Americans, most of us have been raised in a culture of "haves." We are constantly driven by having more. More stuff, more opportunities, and more experiences are what people strive for. In the step of Release, it's very important to consider what our needs and wants are and recognize that sometimes more choices and more stuff do not always make us happier. Listening to your inner guide can make releasing what you don't need easier.

Stop to think for a moment about the number of choices you face in a day relative to the choices your grandparents would have faced in a day. Odds are your grandparent had many fewer choices at the grocery store shelf, fewer options of houses or apartments to live in, and fewer choices of a career. We are blessed but some would say cursed, with the number of choices we have every day.

The typical American view is that choices are good. While it is certainly true that a life without choices is bad, there is a growing body of evidence that in many cases, too much choice is just too much. A certain level of choice is necessary for our happiness, but too much choice can actually decrease our happiness.

Have you heard the story of the famous Draeger's Jam Study? This study is especially meaningful to me because I once lived in the neighborhood where the study was conducted and used to shop at the Draeger's Market where the study was run.

Draeger's is an upscale market in Menlo Park, a couple of miles north of Stanford University. A graduate student at Stanford, Sheena Iyengar wanted to measure the impact of choice on customers' decision-making process. To do this, Iyengar set up two different tables of jam. One set up included six types of jam and the other twelve. Customers were encouraged to taste the jams and given coupons to purchase these jams at a reduced price. While the set up with twelve types of jam attracted slightly more customers to the table to taste the jams, the set up with six jams had a significantly higher purchase rate.

Iyengar's study indicates that while we may be attracted to higher levels of choice, *we are more likely to take action if there are fewer choices*. Similar studies looking at choices in retirement investments, and toasters have shown similar results. We all want choice, but at a certain point, too much choice can be overwhelming and actually drive inaction versus action.

As the number of choices in our lives have increased, so has the rate of American depression. There is a great deal of evidence that the abundance of choice we have in so many circles of our lives today can lead to depression, inaction, and feeling frozen.

What does the abundance of choice have to do with spirituality and job hunting? The enormous abundance of choice in our conscious lives has a direct impact on our subconscious lives. Our subconscious, which is our link to our spiritual self, is, at its core, a relatively simplistic thinker. It can struggle and become overwhelmed when flooded by many inputs and high levels of choice. We need to have a conscious understanding of how so much choice can negatively impact the subconscious and cloud our connection to our true spirit.

There is also a conscious-level impact of the abundance of choice on job hunting. With so many careers, roles, and opportunities out there, choosing wisely what actions to take to prepare and find a job can be difficult. It is easy to get swept up in thinking that you are taking productive actions to find a job, but really your actions are unlikely to bear fruit because of the diffuseness of your activity. It's very natural to feel like you should apply for every job that is somewhat close to your dream. After all, one thing can lead to another, and you certainly don't want to overlook an opportunity or fail to throw your hat in the ring. While that's true, applying to many jobs with the proper attention and approach takes a great deal of time. Only you can decide what opportunities and actions make sense for you.

Release the obsession with choice and refocus on freedom.

RELEASE
ACTIVITIES

WHAT I WILL RELEASE

"Forgiveness is not an emotion. It is a decision made by your whole self after your true emotional work has been done." — Karla McLaren

We all carry a lot of emotional baggage that can get in the way of attracting a new job. To begin the step of Release, we begin with a writing assignment — essentially a list of things you would like to, or need to, release.

Open your journal to a fresh page. List what you want to release. You might choose to begin by listing physical things like clothes that don't fit, or jewelry you never wear. Physical things can be tying up energy or taking up unnecessary space that you don't need. Clean house.

Besides physical things, we all have emotions and experiences that can be released. It's not uncommon for this list to grow and grow, without us even realizing it. Some people will have lots of little things on their list, like letting go of the fact your kid didn't clean his room on time, and some people will have bigger things like a fight last week with the boss. For the purposes of this activities, all of these are fair game.

The first step here is to focus on making the list, not doing the work of releasing. Rattle off what you think of and just add it to the list. Don't worry about processing all of this. Go for quantity and comprehensiveness, not driving this list to a sense of completion.

At some point, you will run out of steam. When that happens, take three deep breaths. If nothing else comes to you, it's time to put down your pen and call the list done.

Read your list. Again, you are not trying to process the feelings or the emotions of each individual line on the list, but to have a sense of just how big this releasing task could be. Pat yourself on the back! Most of us find it a little daunting to make a list of what we are hanging on to. You've done something difficult — a first step toward releasing.

The next step is to review the list. If something feels easy to let go, and you don't need to give it a lot more thought, cross it off the list. Undoubtedly, a few things will feel pretty easy, and you will feel great striking them off the list. Others will be harder.

For the sticky ones, circle them. These are the ones you carry forward and handle with self-hypnosis or meditation.

Take the list of things you want to release, with some items crossed off and others circled. Now you will work on releasing the circled items.

Take yourself into a meditative state through self-hypnosis or meditation. If you need more information or training on how to do this, please see my website at: www.michellewalters.net.

In hypnosis, you will bring to mind one item on your list of things to release. The subconscious likes to keep things easy, so I don't recommend trying to do too many items from your list in the same session.

What you will do with each item on your list is imagine it going away. There are numerous ways to envision this release. I'm going to give you a few choices here which you can choose from. If there is a different visual image that you think works well to release that emotion or event, use it.

Ways to envision releasing an event or emotion:

1. Put it on a tray and hand off the tray to someone else.
2. Wrap it up like a package and mail it.
3. Tie a rock to it and throw it in a deep lake or ocean.
4. Transform it into a wishing dandelion and blow away the seeds.
5. Build a rocket ship and send it into space.
6. Light it up and burn it in a bright flaming blaze.

For each circled item on your list, take at least one full minute to visualize releasing it. As you release items, cross them off your list. If you have a lot of items on your list, split the list into sections and work on a few each day. Releasing takes time; do not feel the need to rush into releasing everything at once.

STEPS:

1. Make a list of all the things you need to release.
2. When you think you are done, take three deep breaths, if nothing comes move on.
3. Read your list. Let go of the easy stuff right away and cross them off. Circle the harder things.
4. Use a meditative or hypnotic state to envision the hard things going away.

A HABIT TO CHANGE

"Progress always involves risk; you can't steal second base and keep your foot on first." — Frederick Wilcox

For this activity, think of a single habit that you do that you can break for just one day. The habit you choose to break does not need to be anything important, and it doesn't have to be difficult to do. Perhaps you will choose to brush your teeth with your other hand, to take a new route to the grocery story, or to eat breakfast for dinner one day. You are welcome to come up with more than one habit to break for a day, but it is only really necessary to choose one.

When you make efforts to break this habit, you are releasing a small bit of energy that was always playing out the same way, to play out a different way. Making this habit-change a conscious choice and recognizing that disturbing the status quo will start the Release powers turning. As you take this alternative action, remind yourself that the purpose of this is to release.

If your action is small you may choose to repeat it for several days. Each time you repeat this new way of doing things, your subconscious mind is recognizing that there is not a single way of doing things and that change can be made.

Write about this experience in your journal.

STEPS:

1. Think about a habit to change.
2. Pick a new action, small or big.
3. Repeat for several days until you feel more flexible.

Keep and Drop

"Chains of habit are too light to be felt until they are too heavy to be broken."
— Warren Buffet

An important part of releasing is letting go of any bad habits, any practices that are not serving you today. This includes bad habits which affect the physical body, like being sedentary or overeating. Even though this is a book about what you need to do on a spiritual level, the physical and spiritual level are connected, and it is important to take care of your physical self too.

For this activity, make two columns in your journal. The left-hand column is for habits you are proud of that you want to keep. The right-hand column is for habits that you want to break or reshape. Title the columns.

Start with habits that are related to your physical body. Be sure to note things you do to take care of your body, like eating regularly or walking or stretching in the left-hand column. Make note of any important physical body habits you want to change in the right-hand column. Don't go overboard. The idea here is to acknowledge if there are things you need to change and release them, either by taking action or by deciding to let them go.

For example, if you regularly eat a healthy breakfast and you like that habit, enter that in the left-hand column. If you have been thinking you should give up sugar, that goes in the right-hand column.

Once you are done making this list for things related to your physical body, draw a line at the bottom of both columns across your page. You may have only a few or many things on your list. Either is fine.

The second step of this activity is to do the same thing with things that are not clearly physical. What habits do you have that you want to keep and what habits do you want to drop? Perhaps you want to remember to consistently thank your coworker for producing a status report on time. Maybe you want to cut yourself more slack when you don't get everything done in a day that you had wanted to do.

Whatever it is, question yourself and see what to add in either the keep or drop column.

After you have finished, reflect upon your work. Notice that you have a number of practices that are clearly positive and you want to keep. In the second column, you have some things that you can choose to release. If you are ready to take the Release step with any of these practices or habits, try to do so in the next week or month.

There are some simple lessons to take away from this activity. First, we all have things to release, big or small, and we all can take action mentally and/or physically to release them. Second, releasing can take time. While it's important to push yourself forward on your job hunt, recognize that not everything can be calendared and don't be too hard on yourself.

STEPS:

1. Make two columns in your journal: habits I am proud of and a habit I want to break.
2. Make a list for the physical habits and then for the non-physical habits.
3. Reflect on your list.
4. Pick a few of the habits you want to release to work on in the next week or month.

CHOOSING WHEN TO CHOOSE

"Learning to choose is hard. Learning to choose well is harder. And learning to choose well in a world of unlimited possibilities is harder still, perhaps too hard."
— Barry Schwartz

As discussed earlier, we have so much choice in our lives that at times it can get in the way of our happiness. Barry Schwartz, in his book *The Paradox of Choice*, has a long list of excellent ideas that can help you navigate our world of constant choices. This activity focuses on just one of those steps and is called "Choosing When to Choose."

Searching for a job is a process with constant choices. What should I be doing to find a job today? Should I contact that person I met a long time ago who might not even remember me? Should I apply for a job if I don't know much about the company? The truth is, there is an endless set of choices about how to conduct your job hunt and the answers are far from clear.

We know that often, we are presented with many choices and that the high number of choices frequently isn't helpful. Having more choices often clouds decision making without improving the quality or value of our choice. One of the most powerful ways to push back on this invisible force is to beef up our strength and *make a conscious decision to make fewer choices.*

The truth is, not every decision matters all that much. Becoming more at ease with consciously choosing to eliminate some choices can improve your sense of well-being.

In your journal, take the following steps:

1. Make a list of a few recent decisions that you have made. The list could include things like a recent purchase, a retirement plan allocation, or a relationship change. You may include work related decisions, but also include at least one other decision that was not solely about work.

2. For each one of those decisions, list what it took to make that decision. List the steps, research, time, anxiety and effort that went into making each decision.

3. Notice how it felt to do the work of step 2.

4. In conclusion, ask yourself how your decision benefitted from doing the work you listed in step 2.

5. Pick a few of the habits you want to release to work on in the next week or month.

It's highly likely that this activity will help you realize that at least some of your recent decisions had you spending a lot of time in the analytic and consideration phase that didn't provide that much value. Maybe some of your decisions would benefit from a rule of thumb — like don't push yourself to visit multiple grocery stores every week just to pick up a single favorite item, or don't be angry at yourself for asking for help with difficult tasks.

Are there any takeaways you can use to simplify your job hunt? You might decide to make some rules of thumb for yourself, like to make it a practice to phone people the day after an unanswered email, or to always wait 24 hours to send a thank you note, to ensure the hiring manager is still thinking about you the next day. Whatever practices you can set up for yourself that help eliminate excess choice can do a lot to make you feel better about your hunt and spend your time productively.

CREATE

CREATE

"Hitch your wagon to a star." — Ralph Waldo Emerson

Creating is my favorite part of manifesting a new job. I love to spend time imagining what my new job will be and how it will feel to do it. All steps on the Manifestation Wheel are necessary, but the Create step is very special and has a particular kind of energy.

We all came to earth to have the experience of creation. Starting in childhood, we played games, imagined friends, and tried new things. These activities were the beginning of a lifetime of creation activities.

Some people have jobs that don't feel very creative. That might even be why you are seeking a new job. While the balance between more and less creative tasks can vary widely from job to job, almost all jobs in our society today call for some level of creativity. In our best jobs, our creativity has room to shine forth.

Creating a new job is all about seeing it in your mind. This chapter and the following activities are all designed to help you see your new job with clarity and purpose.

Why Create, Not Ask

"In the middle of difficulty lies opportunity." — Albert Einstein

Many spiritual teachers call this step in the Manifestation Wheel "Ask" versus "Create." Let me explain why I think Create is a more appropriate term.

When we use the word "Ask," we are typically thinking of something very specific. I ask my son to do the dishes and I ask someone if I can pass by their cart in the supermarket. The word Ask suggests that what you are stating as the object of your desire is one exact thing. That's true in the case of getting the dishes done or passing a cart, but it's not necessarily true when you are looking for a job. Odds are there are several jobs that would be a good fit for you. To think of this step as Asking is too narrow a focus. A broader focus will serve you better.

Another reason why I prefer the term Create is that the word Ask implies that there is no making involved. Ask suggests that there is a list of available items in inventory at the store that sells jobs. Instead, there is constant flux in what jobs are available. The idea that you are creating your job feels more in keeping with a changing set of opportunities and the constant state of energy in motion.

Last, I find the word Ask disempowering. Ask suggests that you, the seeker, are purely a recipient. "Create" carries power that Ask does not. If you think about this step as Create, you are taking ownership of the work involved. Manifesting a new job is work at both a physical and spiritual level. Put your skin in the game and focus on creating so as to take a very active approach.

GENERAL VERSUS SPECIFIC

"Balance is not something you find, it's something you create."
— Jana Kingsford

One of the hardest parts of creating the image of your right next job is working out how specific versus how general to imagine it. It can be very tempting to lock-in to imagining yourself in a particular position at a particular firm and devoting lots of mental energy and time toward that dream. I have done this many times.

A few years ago, I came across an open corporate role for a coffee company in my area. They were looking for someone with my expertise in marketing. I was so excited about the position. The location was good and the salary was solid. This was a brand of coffee I really adored. I had many years of experience in the field, including work for another coffee manufacturer. For several weeks, I spent time imagining doing this job and feeling like it was the one.

Well, I didn't get the job. I don't know why they passed on my candidacy. Perhaps I was overqualified or looked like the manager's ex-girlfriend. I have no idea. Regardless, the Universe didn't deliver this job to me, even though I had been mentally believing, with the full force of my creation energy, that I would get this job. The Universe had something else in mind.

What you have to do in mentally imagining the right job is tricky. You have to *balance specificity with generality*. Instead of putting all your energy into a single opportunity, put your energy into a more general feeling that the right job will come along and it will feel great. See this like a digital map — one where you can zoom out and zoom in. Both levels of the map represent the same thing at different levels of detail. Balance high and low.

While you may think on a conscious level that you know exactly what the right job is for you, it is important to remember that your conscious mind doesn't know everything. The subconscious and superconscious are part of making a great job match. Recall that

Kahneman's advice on making decisions is to do a thorough analysis first, then lean on your intuition. Don't give in to the temptation to visualize deeply on a single opportunity. It is too narrow a view.

ADVANTAGE HAPPINESS

"Most folks are about as happy as they make up their minds to be."
— Abraham Lincoln

In Shawn Achor's book, *The Happiness Advantage,* Achor stresses how positivity attracts success. Curiously, he comes just one step shy of observing how similar this viewpoint is to the premise of the law of attraction, which states that you attract what you believe.

In *The Happiness Advantage*, Achor argues that in opposition to how many of us have been taught to think, happiness doesn't follow success, *happiness comes first*. It's not the success of getting a good job that brings happiness — happiness is what brings the new job and the success. The equation is flipped. Achor offers considerable evidence for this, including a study of nuns, which showed that the happiest nuns lived longer than the less happy initiates.

The study observed the same individuals at different times in their lives. The researchers looked at 180 Catholic nuns, all born before 1917, and found that happiness in youth was correlated with longer life spans. All of the nuns had composed autobiographical journal entries when they entered the convent. Researchers coded these journals for their level of positivity. What they found was that by age 85, 90 percent of the happiest quartile of nuns were still alive, compared to only 34 percent of the least happy quartile. Since none of the nuns would have known at the time of their initiation how long they were going to live, this is highly suggestive that a positive outlook leads to a longer life.

Another longitudinal study, this time of men, supports the belief that love and social relationships are the ticket to a happy and successful life. The Harvard Men study, which began in the 1930s and continues today, followed 268 men throughout their lives, tracking physical health, relationships, and work histories. Their findings show strong evidence that social relationships and love are what makes a man successful. The notion that happiness follows success is not supported.

Can happiness prevent the common cold? A study suggests it might. Researchers surveyed participants to measure their level of happiness, then injected them with the virus for the common cold. What happened? The individuals who were happier fought off the virus much better than the less happy individuals. Doctors that met with the participants and measured their symptoms — sneezing, inflammation, coughing, and congestion, saw the differences.

What do these stories have in common? All of them support the viewpoint that *people who are happy draw success to themselves*, versus success leading to happiness. Happiness is something we can focus on and produce in ourselves.

Achor's audience is broad and probably somewhat academic, and he stays away from a spiritual interpretation of his data. However, it cannot be overlooked that he is using a material, rational, scientific approach to research what makes people feel "happy."

"Happy" is a feeling. It is a state of spirit. Achor's conclusion that happiness brings success gives weight to the argument that there is a spiritual component, the feeling of happiness, in bringing about success. There are scientific markers that can evidence someone is happy like levels of oxytocin and dopamine, but the definition of happiness is so much more than we can measure with a blood test or a microscope. Achor actually is compiling evidence for the law of attraction, even though he doesn't call it that.

I am a very positive person, and my positivity has absolutely helped me on the job front. Before I attended graduate school, I worked for a decision analysis consulting company on Sand Hill Road in Palo Alto. My initial job there was attending very high-level consulting meetings and assisting the partners of the firm with meeting facilitation and recording. I loved playing even a small part in these important meetings and I was fortunate enough to get opportunities to travel extensively domestically and some overseas in this role. Because I was good at my job, positive, and adaptable, I was offered a short-term role in New Zealand and another role managing the company office in London. When I returned from London, I received a promotion, working in Palo Alto as a Business Analyst. I was very fortunate to have all of these opportunities. They were brought on by the happiness I had in doing a job well and being proud of my accomplishments.

WHAT MAKES CREATING HARD

"Ask and it shall be given you." — Jesus

The Create step can be tough for many reasons including
- Managing time.
- Feeling lonely.
- Knowing what to focus on.
- Maintaining that focus.
- Knowing your status and progress.
- Incomplete release.

Managing time and feeling lonely are two reasons people have trouble with the Create step. For many of us who have worked in offices with multiple teammates, being out of work can feel especially lonely. In an office environment you have other people around to help make the time go by. At home alone, looking for a job, the hours can seem to sometimes drag on forever — though occasionally they fly by. Workplaces provide many of us with valuable social interactions that can be missing if you are seeking a job from home by yourself.

If you are working and looking for a job at the same time, it's likely you also have this sense of loneliness. Generally, you can't be forthright about your job search with your current employer and finding a way to keep your job-hunting activities on the down-low takes energy and may feel dishonest. Either way, to be successful at the Create step, you must allow any feelings of loneliness to pass through you and drift away. You don't have to be an amazing time manager, but you do need to find ways to maintain your attention and stay on task if you want to attract a new job.

Another reason people struggle in the Create task is knowing what to focus on. While some job seekers start their job hunt very clear about exactly what title they want, many others are not as clear. Because jobs change so rapidly now, what one job was called a couple of years ago is not necessarily what it might be called today. Within my experience, I have seen all kinds of jobs with titles that didn't fit and written job descriptions that didn't match what the hiring team described verbally. With considerable chaos in the job-hunting world, it can be very difficult to know how to focus your energy.

Creating can be difficult for some people because it can be such an open-ended step. It is easy to get lost in the step of Create, always imagining new things and never really focusing on anything specific. If the Universe hears from you that you want three different kinds of jobs, it won't know which one to bring you. If creating feels difficult, make sure you are focused on what you want the Universe to bring you.

As businesspeople, we are accustomed to measuring progress on our projects. Measuring the progress on creating your new job is filled with uncertainty. While it is important to keep records of your leads, contacts, and opportunities, it can be very difficult to know exactly where you stand in a hiring process. Sometimes the hiring company will be very clear about the process and timing, and sometimes they won't be, maybe because things come up and they don't know either.

Releasing, the step before creating, is a big step and it can take time. Many times I have done some of my releasing work and proceeded to try creating a job before I was ready. It can be extremely tempting to want to skip or skimp on releasing and get to creating. Releasing can be really hard and even mentally or emotionally painful. If you are having problems focusing on what to create, step back and make sure you are in a good place and haven't neglected the work necessary to release.

When my husband passed in April 2011, I was out of work. My company had laid me off a couple of months before he died. While I was thankful to have more space for grieving, being out of work meant I had a lot of time on my hands to be sad and not distracted by work. I started looking for work seriously in July, but I was unable to get anywhere with my job hunt for months. As I said before, everything going on in your life is related. In hindsight, I can see that I needed more time to process his death and release. An excellent opportunity came my way in February 2012 and I was very thankful to get back to work.

With these challenges, it can be tough to feel like you are on target and making headway as you seek to Create your new job. The activities at the end of this section are meant to help you focus and be comfortable with your efforts and progress.

CREATE
ACTIVITIES

PIGGY-BACK OFF THE SUCCESS OF OTHERS

"Life is either a daring adventure or nothing at all."
— Helen Keller

To kick off the Create step activities of the Manifestation Wheel, we will start by observing what people around you have manifested.

Are there stories from your family that evidence someone successfully fulfilling a dream? Perhaps a grandparent who emigrated to the US and went to medical school or started a business? Do you have a sibling who dreamed of finding a soulmate and has been happily married for years? If we pause to think and look around, we can all think of someone, probably many someones, who brought something into being that started with a dream and came to be.

It is important that as you think about these stories to realize that, with few exceptions, they are not miracles. Most of these examples of manifestation required physical steps, maybe many difficult physical steps over years, to come together. Again, the process of manifesting absolutely requires alignment on the physical plane and takes effort. Look at Oprah. Oprah has succeeded in manifesting a tremendous media empire and attributes much of her success to her spirit. She did not make a media empire without going to work, hiring people, and working really hard on the physical plane. Expect that work on the physical plane is necessary, work guided by your spirit and you will be on track.

In your journal, write down one or two of these stories from friends and family. Take a few paragraphs to describe who did the manifesting, and what work they did on the physical plane and the spiritual plane (if you know) to achieve their dream.

When you have finished, re-read your entries. Imagine being the person who manifested a dream — where they were, what they struggled with, and how they succeeded.

STEPS:

1. List a few people in your life who have successfully fulfilled a dream.
2. Pick a few to write about in more depth. Write down their stories in detail.
3. Re-read the entries and imagine being the person who made all this happen.

WHAT HAVE YOU ATTRACTED?

"What you think you become.
What you feel you attract.
What you imagine, you create."
— Buddha

Critical to your success at manifesting a great job or anything else is believing you can.

This can be incredibly difficult when things seem to be going the wrong way. If you lost your job, it can feel impossible to believe that you will find another job. This is another place that cognitive biases can slip into the picture. Both the availability (recency) bias and the negativity bias work to make you feel like you won't be successful finding a job. Nevertheless, you must put yourself in a mindset that not only is a new job possible, it is actually inevitable. It will feel like a trick you are playing on your mind. It is the right thing to do.

If this is the case, you likely need to revisit the Release step. Releasing can be particularly difficult when you have lost your job and things seem to be going the wrong way. The steps are flexible and you may need to go back from time to time to work on a previous step.

One of the best ways to move forward the Create process is to build your subconscious and conscious awareness that *you* have succeeded at manifesting in the past. In building this awareness, you build your ability to believe that you played a part in receiving good things in the past, making it all the more believable that you can do it again and receive more good things in the future.

To do this, you will need the ability to give yourself credit. You need to see yourself as an active player in your life and recognize that things you dreamed about coming true, did.

Through this manifesting process, I have received numerous wonderful gifts from the Universe. I have attracted a house, many jobs, loving partners, and a beautiful son. Think about what you have manifested.

Many people fall into a trap of visualizing what they want, and then opening their eyes and seeing that it is not there yet. They allow the (current) absence of their dream on the physical plane to shake their belief that their energy can attract their desires. This disturbs the attraction process and causes the person to lose the belief and headway they were making.

One of the best ways to charge up your ability to not just turn but spin the Manifestation Wheel is to notice what you have already attracted. In noticing what you have attracted in the past, you amp up your ability to believe that you can attract more wonderful things. This is a fun activity because you will get the chance to remember wonderful things that have happened in your past and give yourself credit for them.

꙳

Relax and find a comfortable place to sit. You are going to take yourself into a light state of hypnosis, essentially a meditative state so that your memories are enhanced and extra vivid.

Call forth a memory of something good that happened in your life. It can be big or small. You might recall receiving a special gift for a birthday or a trip to a restaurant for dinner with friends. If your spouse was unexpectedly kind recently, that would work too.

Hold an image of that pleasant memory in your mind. Next, you are going to think about events, things, or memories that are related to your pleasant memory. Perhaps you told the friend who gave you the wonderful gift how much you liked that item. Revive this pleasant memory and notice other associated memories.

Next, pause for a moment and realize that even if you know a lot about what made this happy event come together, you cannot know everything. For example, why had it come up that you liked that particular item earlier, when you were speaking with your friend? How was it that friends who are often unavailable were able to make that particular dinner party? What made your spouse be extra kind that day?

We never know everything about why something happens. There are always more questions than we can answer. Not everything is knowable.

Go back to your journal and write a few sentences reflecting on your experience.

STEPS:

1. Relax and find a comfortable place to sit.
2. Call forth a memory of something good that happened in your life.
3. Hold an image of that pleasant memory in your mind.
4. Notice the associated memories.
5. Realize that the path to this wonderful memory is unknowable.
6. Write a few sentences in your journal about the experience.

IMAGINE YOUR DREAM JOB

*"I am enough of an artist to draw freely upon my
imagination. Imagination is more important than knowledge.
Knowledge is limited. Imagination encircles the world."*
— Albert Einstein

Take out the crayons, markers and colored pencils! It's time for a little arts and crafts!

Unlike the activities you have done so far, this one is about art. Why? Because art is an excellent way of expressing who you are and what you want to bring into this life.

The creation step includes imagining many different aspects of your new job. It can include imagining getting ready for work, the commute, your desk, and your colleagues. It includes dreaming about parts of the work you find fun and feel more like play than work. Creating includes imagining the kinds of conversations you will have with your coworkers, clients and others. The Create step is where you find what a great job would feel like and hold on to that feeling as long and as often as you can. In sitting in this space of feeling the new good job, you will attract it to you.

This activity uses artwork to visualize. The mind is very visual, and by feeding it pictures, it learns more about what you are creating and the feeling of that creation.

Like the writing activities you have already done, the artwork in this activity is a pre-step to the reflection and meditation on the art you make.

֍

First, spend a moment visualizing the space. Are there clocks on the wall? Do you sit alone or with others? Do you see plants or windows? Imagining what your workplace will look like on a physical level is helpful as a means to open up your subconscious mind and your spirit to what you feel like in this workplace. Next, draw a picture or pictures of yourself at your dream job. If you work at a desk, draw your desk. Are there other desks in close proximity? Draw them. Are you in an office environment? Perhaps you are in a home office. Draw the place where you see yourself working most of the time.

You might find yourself drawing a single page, or you might find yourself picking up a second or third piece of paper to draw other scenes associated with the new job. If you feel moved to draw the building you work in, go ahead. Feel like drawing a chart of where you sit in the organization? Go for it.

The idea here is to open your mind visually to what you wish to create as a pre-step to raising the feeling within you of having this wonderful job. In this activity, it is important not to get too hung up on the specific versus general. It's not uncommon to feel that what you drew in your picture should be exactly like your next workplace, and to feel anything not an exact match is wrong. I have received jobs that looked just like my picture, but more often they haven't. It's not the accuracy of the picture that matters. It is the *ability of the picture to help you visualize and raise the feeling* of having your next job.

As you did with your writing activities, your next step is to reflect upon your picture in a state of meditation or self-hypnosis. This part of the activity is important because in the activation of your subconscious, you raise your internal energy — the energy which draws opportunities to you.

Bring yourself into the alpha meditative state. Remember, it is completely possible to have your eyes open and remain in this relaxed state. Look at your picture and then visualize it in your mind. Try animating your image in hypnosis and exploring it. In this state of mind you have the power to do all kinds of things. You might look at your computer to see what kind of a computer you have or open your desk drawers or even read your first email at your new job, welcoming you and introducing you to the organization. There is no limit to what you can visualize.

This activity is at the heart of the Create step of the Manifestation Wheel. It is so important, I recommend you repeat the visualization portion of it many times. Once you have completed your first rotation of the Manifestation Wheel, if you seek to accelerate the turn into more of a spin, repeat this activity frequently.

STEPS:

1. Draw one or more pictures of your dream job.
2. Using an alpha meditative state, visualize this scene in your subconscious mind.
3. Repeat, using the same or different pictures of your dream job.

ADAM I AND ADAM II

"When you are able to maintain your own highest standards of integrity — regardless of what others may do — you are destined for greatness."
— Napoleon Hill

David Brooks, Commentator and New York Times writer, wrote a book called *The Road to Character*. In this book he references Joseph Soloveitchik, an American Orthodox rabbi who wrote an essay in 1965 titled "The Lonely Man of Faith." Soloveitchik was descended from a long line of rabbis. He was born in present day Belarus and received his Ph.D. in epistemology and metaphysics from the University of Berlin.

Soloveitchik described two different "Adams" that characterize two sides of our human nature. The first Adam, Adam I, was a man based on resumé virtues: skills you bring to the marketplace — how to build, how to create, how to innovate and transform. He is a worldly, ambitious person, defined by what he does.

Your resumé captures these values and should showcase them in a form that makes you proud. Since your resumé is so important in its function as your introduction and differentiator, it is critical that both its content and appearance resonate with who you are. Make sure you are taking the necessary steps on the physical track to have a resumé which does you justice, looks good, and makes you proud.

Adam II, the second Adam, is a man based on eulogy virtues. Adam II wants to please God. He wants to do good and be good and to live in a way that honors creation and possibilities. He is unconcerned with making things and instead concerned with being virtuous.

Every one of us is part Adam I and part Adam II. Often in the course of looking for a job and living our everyday lives, we find ourselves wrapped up in focusing on our Adam I traits. The necessity of communicating our skills and experience is important to getting a job. But think about it; resumés don't include how you cheered up the kids on the losing team. Resumés leave out how you came through for your family when no one else wanted to host a holiday dinner. Resumés don't tell the story of when you consoled a valued, frustrated co-worker and convinced them to stick with the organization. While these kinds of acts are not what most employers look for on a resumé, they are critical to what defines a man or woman.

When you're looking for a job, don't fall into the trap of thinking you are what you see on your resumé. You are so much more than that.

$$\wp$$

For this activity, you are going to work on your Adam II eulogy virtues. It's time to take a short break from working on your resumé and instead think about who you are from another perspective.

How do you want people to remember you? Who are you as a person? What are the traits that don't belong on a resumé, but are fundamentally part of who you are?

Make a list in your journal of as many of these traits, actions and accomplishments as you can. You are making a list of your eulogy virtues, virtues that don't appear on resumés. Unlike your resumé, which needs to be easy to understand and public, this list is just for you. Bullets work well. Try to come up with five, and after you get to five, go for ten. Make as long a list or as short a list as you please. Some people find it hard to see the good in themselves, so going a little slower and only trying to list a few things is an easier way to get started.

When you are finished, take note of what you have included. Notice if this activity reveals any other sources or connections you might reach out to about your job hunt. It may also surface traits and characteristics or experiences worthy of incorporating in your resumé. It is critical that in the process of your job hunt you do not lose track that what you present to potential employers is only a partial view of yourself. You are much more than your resumé and this activity will show you how very true that is.

STEPS:

1. Make a list in your journal of as many of these eulogy traits, actions, and accomplishments as you can.
2. When you have finished, read what you wrote.
3. Are there traits that surprised you and might be useful?
4. Are there people or connections you might want to reach out to?

BE EXPECTANT

"May you never be too grown up to search the skies on Christmas Eve." — Unknown

It is important to live in a positive state. While we all have our bad days and our ordeals, it is critical to keep the mind focused as positively as possible, so that we may attract opportunities and good into our lives.

This activity is about being expectant. It will help you build excitement and confidence in your ability to get a new job. As the energy within you grows, it will work like a magnet to draw in the people and connections you need for the Universe to deliver a spiritually appropriate new job.

The first step is to think of something that you know is coming that excites you. It doesn't matter what it is. If something coming up is very exciting for you, like maybe a major outing or completing a major accomplishment, that will work great for this activity.

It is ideal to think of something that you expect within the next ten days. You want to see this as something that is a sure thing and a soon thing.

Write down the object of your expectancy in your journal, and then below it, add a few bullets about the details and then a few about how you feel about receiving this gift or event.

Your notebook may look something like this:

"Going out for dinner Saturday night with Janet."

Details:
- Eating at Cafe Claude, my favorite restaurant.
- May order the Clam Chowder or the Steak.
- May treat myself to a glass of sparkling white wine.

Feelings:
- Happiness to get to visit with Janet after a long time.
- Love the taste of a delicious meal, especially when prepared by someone else.
- I enjoy the view from restaurant of the waterfront.

Once you have completed that list, start a new paragraph below the list. In this paragraph, write as if you have already received this gift or event. Here's another example of what this might look like in your notebook:

> *"Already received the dinner."*
>
> *"Last night, Janet and I went to Cafe Claude. I hadn't seen her in over 3 months, and she had so much news to share. It's unbelievable how quickly the kids are growing up!"*
>
> *"We had an excellent table with a view of the bay. Much to my surprise, there was a special risotto that I couldn't pass up. It was absolutely delicious, and I really enjoyed my glass of champagne. Seeing and connecting with Janet this week, at such a wonderful place, made me happy and grateful."*

At this point, you have built expectancy at the conscious level because you have written about it. The second part of the activity is to build expectancy at the subconscious level.

For part two, write down a second gift or event that you expect to happen within the next ten days or so. It is important it be a completely different event than the one you used in part one. You are going to work on this one in a relaxed state of self-hypnosis.

Next, bring yourself into that relaxed state. While you are deeply relaxed, bring this upcoming event into your mind. Just as you did at the conscious level, flesh out the upcoming event and imagine it in great detail. Imagine the event with details like the temperature, the weather, sounds or tastes that apply. The more real the event, the better.

Build up the feelings in your mind associated with the event. Imagine how you feel with this going on. Make the feelings as real as possible. When you feel strongly as if the event has already happened, give thanks for it and end your session.

STEPS:

1. Choose an upcoming event you are excited about and write it in your journal.
2. Imagine possible positive associated events and write them down in bullets.
3. Write a statement as if the event has already occurred.
4. Write a short paragraph consisting of your bullets as if these positive events already happened.
5. Meditate or do self-hypnosis to imagine this event as in the past with the positive associated experiences.

Logos and Your Intuition

*"Your smile is your logo, your personality is your business
card; how you leave others feeling after an experience with
you becomes your trademark."*
— Jay Danzle

Symbols are powerful in your subconscious. Your subconscious saves memories and associations frequently as symbols. Symbols can be powerful tools to help you create and to recognize what matches with your spirit and what doesn't.

Brands, logos and mission statements are all symbolic shortcuts. While it might sound weird, these symbols have an energy to themselves. I find it easiest to think about logos, but the same can be said for the brands, tag lines, and mission statements as well. The brand logo for Shell Oil has a different energy than the brand logo for FedEx. Even the brand logo for Wells Fargo has a different energy from Bank of America.

To make matters even more interesting, my resonance with a brand may be similar to yours, or it may be a little different. Brands strive to have a singular identity, but, inevitably, when it comes to how an individual relates to them, it can be different. For example, I have a close friend who is a major brand advocate of a bank I do not like. His relationship to the brand is positive and mine is negative. This is what I mean by saying we all have different resonances with the same brands.

Even very small organizations have imagery associated with them — like where their offices are on a map, a photo of the founder, projects they have completed, or customers they have served. If you are seeking work for a small organization that doesn't have the same symbolic shortcuts as a large organization, you may need to adapt this activity to use alternative imagery.

When I am looking for a job, one tool I consistently use is a "Logo Opportunity Chart." This activity will explain how to make and use the Logo Opportunity Chart.

The activity begins by tracking the companies you are interested in working for, which you are probably already doing as part of the physical work necessary to get a job. I usually have a spreadsheet of the companies and individuals I have talked to with the names of opportunities, most recent contact date and various notes about the process.

As part of my research, I look up information on the company, including people I might be working with, the company mission statement, (if they publish one), tag lines, and other information that gives me a better sense of the *emotional* character of the brand. Of course, as part of your due diligence for job hunting at the physical level, you will probably also be researching the company's financials, history, and other more hard data aspects. This activity is to develop your sense of who the brand is as if it was a person with a spirit — who are they really?

$$\wr$$

For this activity, you will collect the logos of the various companies you are interested in pursuing and put them on a single page or slide. If you are pursuing work with organizations too small to have logos, you can substitute pictures of their founders or choose symbols that represent them. This should be a little bit of an art activity in that you want to make the page visually pleasing. Make all of the brand logo images similar in size.

My preference for this activity is to do it on the computer, but it could certainly be done by printing logos and putting them on a board, or even redrawing the logos on a piece of paper. Any of these methods will convey the energy of these different opportunities into a single picture.

When you are done, print out the logo sheet and have a look at it. Your next step will be to go deep inside yourself via self-hypnosis and more deeply sense the energies you associate with each brand logo.

Relax and let your conscious mind slip away to make space for your subconscious mind. In this relaxed alpha state, look again at your Logo Opportunity Chart. Notice if any of the logos seem to recede or if any of them grow bigger. Put your hand over them and notice if any are warm or cold. Are there any that don't feel like they belong? This portion of the activity is meant to allow your intuition to speak to you about the opportunities.

After a few minutes, when you feel you have received any guidance that is going to come, gently return to your waking state.

This activity can help you to prioritize where you should be putting your energy for your job hunt. If, during your alpha state, you observed that some of the logos were receding, held less energy, or were cold or uninteresting, move them down on your list. Your intuition is suggesting that they should receive less of your time and attention. For any logos that were warm, grew bigger, seemed to take a place of importance, or generally felt like they wanted your attention, move those opportunities higher on your priority list.

Because your target opportunities will change over the course of your job hunt, feel free to update your logo opportunity chart and repeat this activity. After you repeat this activity a few times, it will be easier to feel the energies of the logos.

STEPS:

1. Collect logos or small images representing opportunities.
2. Bring yourself into hypnosis and gently reflect on the images, noticing if they stand out, recede or change in any way.
3. After making your observations, consider consciously if you will integrate the feelings that came up into your job hunt priorities.

VISITING WORKPLACES

"Not all those who wander are lost." — J.R.R. Tolkien

If you have the opportunity to visit prospective workplaces, I recommend doing so, preferably prior to meeting the people who work there or going inside for an interview. Being in the physical space of an organization will give you a great deal of both conscious and subconscious feelings about your fit there.

If it's not possible to visit the organization in real life, you can visit them virtually. Look at the office building in Google Maps. Sometimes you can find pictures of the interior of offices. Review pictures of the employees on the organization's page or LinkedIn. The purpose of this activity is to mix the energy of the firms you are pursuing with your own, so that the Universe can review the potential match and put steps in motion if there is a spiritual match to be made with you and a particular opportunity.

Be sure to do this for multiple opportunities. As I mentioned earlier, it is imperative not to allow yourself to be so specific in your imagining of opportunities that you can't see yourself in different places and different jobs. Keep your mind open.

STEPS (Real Life):

1. Locate job site.
2. Visit job site.
3. Reflect on job site, including imagining yourself going to work at this location.

STEPS (Virtual):

1. Research job deeply, viewing sites, images of colleagues, job reports.
2. Reflect on job in a meditative state, imagining yourself experiencing this job.

THANK

THANK

"The deepest craving of human nature is the need to be appreciated."
— William James

If I had an easy, free technique that had been clinically proven to improve both your physical and mental well-being, would you use it? There is one and it is called gratitude. Research on gratitude has shown it can lower blood pressure and improve immune function. People who keep gratitude journals have been shown to sleep one half hour more every night and exercise 33 percent more than those who are not keeping journals. The evidence is there; gratitude is good for your body.

Gratitude also has broad positive influences on mental well-being. Gratitude has been shown to increase feelings of connectedness and altruism, as well as improve relationships. The positive associations related to gratitude are too numerous to list here but include improved feelings of energy, improved ability to cope with stress, elevated self-worth and self-confidence, and a greater sense of purpose and resilience.

So, if it's so good for you, why are so many people so thankless? Gratitude is a habit you cultivate. It's like a garden. You have to put work into it and over time the garden gives back.

Humanity has a cognitive bias where we tend to retain the negative and deflect the positive. This was helpful in a world where we were commonly the prey, but it serves us poorly in our highly developed social world. It is important to acknowledge this tendency, our cognitive negativity bias, so that we can mentally notice when we are overlooking our gifts and neglecting an opportunity for gratitude.

What do we know about gratitude and the brain? The study of gratitude in neuroscience is in its infancy. Scientists believe that the neurotransmitter dopamine is necessary for the perception and expression of gratitude. Early work suggests that the left prefrontal cortex may be related to the feeling of gratitude. The left prefrontal cortex is also associated with love and compassion.

Gratitude is partly hereditary. Studies have estimated the heritability of gratitude at about 40 percent. This implies that while your parents have a lot to do with your expression of gratitude, the bulk of your gratitude comes from somewhere besides your genes. Gratitude is a habit you cultivate. It's not just about how you were born.

I think part of what makes gratitude so helpful is that to be grateful, you have to consider two sides. Whether you are thanking a person for something they did or thanking a deity or higher power for something, the fact is there is another presence in the gratitude equation that is outside the self. Gratitude requires a receiver, a gift, and a giver. Putting someone else in the spotlight as the giver is a sharing of energy across the Universe.

One of the things I find most interesting and exciting about gratitude is that research has shown that gratitude can propel itself. Expressing gratitude makes it easier to express more gratitude. Isn't that wonderful! Envisioning gratitude as a garden again, it's as if seeing the plants come up makes you want to plant more seeds.

Research has also shown that there are advantages to writing down your blessings versus just thinking them. The act of writing pushes you to organize your thinking and to process the thought at a different level than strictly through thinking. This is one of the major reasons gratitude journals are so highly recommended. The research is there — writing about your gratitude is good for you.

PRACTICE GIVING THANKS

"If you count all your assets, you always show a profit."
— Robert Quillen

To receive a new job, practice giving thanks. Become an expert at giving thanks on the physical level and recognizing the many gifts and positive energy exchanges between friends, family, neighbors, workmates and colleagues. Make the time to give thanks for many other occasions that are outside of what we see in our material existence.

Some of these include:

- Gifts from the Universe like sunshine, rain and happiness.
- Synchronicities like when someone you are thinking of calls you out of the blue.
- Unexpected things like a machine working when it might have failed.

When you give thanks for things that seem to come from the Universe, several things happen. First, you place your body and mind in the energy of gratitude, which we know is a healing, peace-making and productive energy. Second, you build your belief in the power of the spirit by acting as if it exists. Third, this kind of gratitude acts as a catalyst toward bringing your desires into being. Thanking the Universe is a very positive and worthwhile action to take. How do you say thank you for things that are when you don't know why they are or where they came from? It's simple. You just do. This is an occasion where what you want to do is notice something and then say thank you for it. You don't want to think too much or ask why. Just say thank you.

If the sun is shining, pair the thought "Oh, look how pretty, the sun is shining," with "Thank you Universe, for such beautiful sunshine today." If you are feeling happy, notice the feeling and think to yourself, "Thank you Universe, for this good feeling of happiness." If you pay attention, you will find dozens or even a hundred different occasions to slip in these thank you thoughts as the day passes. Each one of these thoughts is healing, builds your belief in the power of spirit, and works as a catalyst for your desires.

I find it's not too big of a stretch to open the mind up to thanking the Universe for good weather, and many people even do this unconsciously. We walk out the door and think, "oh how nice," but don't realize we are actually giving thanks and can formulate it more consciously. But, many people in our physically minded world today find it much less natural to say thank you for synchronicities and unexpected things. Because we are so focused on the physical matter of the Universe, it's common to resist giving thanks for things when we don't know why or how they came to be. My experience is that the more thanking you can manage, even for things that don't feel natural to say thank you for, the more you are developing your spiritual power. All of these moments are opportunities to practice being thankful and we should not let them go by as missed opportunities. When it comes to synchronicities and the unexpected, some people find it strange to say thank you because they get too much in their head and spend time wondering why or how something just happened. Of course there are times when it is beneficial to understand why or how something happened, but sometimes that's overthinking it. There is room in life to simply be thankful for synchronicities and unexpected events. We don't have to understand them to be thankful.

Express gratitude as life moves along. Positivity will help you. During your day, notice when good things happen and give thanks. If your favorite beverage is on sale at the market, think "Thank you." If the clock battery dies and you have an extra one in the drawer, thank yourself for thinking ahead. It is impossible to be too thankful.

Now for the advanced lesson: give thanks not only for events in the present, but also the past and the future. While we have talked about time being an illusion, really living life like time is something other than unidirectional is terribly difficult in our modern age. It sounds completely irrational to say that time isn't linear. And yet we know that Einstein's work indicates that this is true.

If it's hard to imagine saying thank you for things in the future now, that's fine. Instead start by saying thank you for things that happened in the past, even the distant past. Try saying thank you for the days your grandmother took you to feed the ducks when you were a child. Or say thank you for getting into a good college many years ago. Saying thank you for things in the past may feel weird at first, but it should feel good and help you break any notions you have that it is only appropriate to say thank you for things happening today.

Once you've gotten used to saying thank you for things in the past, you want to move on to the hard one — saying thank you for things in your future. Start by saying thank you for something in the near future you are confident about, and to make it easier still, make it something small. For example, try saying thank you today to the Universe for your coffee tomorrow morning. Or saying thank you for having gas in the gas tank next weekend to take you on a special trip. What is in your near future that you can say thank you for today? The goal of this activity is to trick your brain into being comfortable with saying thank you for things you have not yet received.

When you are ready, go for the big one. Say thank you to the Universe for your new job. Do this with meaning and gusto. "Thank you, Universe, for my new job. My new job is fulfilling in every way. I am filled with gratitude for the wonderful job given to me." If you have worked your way up to this, it won't feel so weird. Being thankful for your new job is a critical step in turning the Manifestation Wheel. Land that new job by being thankful it has already arrived.

Over the course of my life, I have put out some big asks. One of the biggest asks I made of the Universe was for a lung transplant for my husband.

My husband Bruce was born with cystic fibrosis (CF). When he was 11 years old and recently diagnosed with CF, he observed that there were no CF patients at the pulmonologist's office over the age of 20. Things did not look good at that point.

Nevertheless, Bruce wanted to be active. As the oldest of five boys with a Dad in the Air Force and a devoted Catholic Mom at home, Bruce kept up with his peers, getting into college, receiving his Eagle Scout Badge and going on to graduate school. Bruce had a passion for Engineering and received a Bachelor's and a Master's degree in Mechanical Engineering from U.T. Arlington.

Before I came along, Bruce met his first wife in engineering school, and they married soon after graduation. Soon they had the standards of the American dream, a house, two cars, and a son and a daughter. However, their marriage fell apart. I met Bruce a couple of years later when we were working at the same company in Texas.

Bruce had survived into his middle age somehow. He wasn't all that spiritual on the surface, but he had an old soul. Bruce was incredibly determined. In the most graceful way, Bruce knew how to naturally balance a fierce determination and adherence to his medical regime with a blasé "doesn't matter, things are good and getting better" kind of attitude toward life. He had the recipe for a secret sauce of living, despite a terminal illness and terrible, scar-filled lungs.

When Bruce and I met and fell in love, he was nearing the end of his rope. While he was well enough to work full time, we would take weekend road trips and need to pull over to run IVs in a port in his arm to cure systemic infections at highway rest stops. He once asked me to pull cash out of his wallet in the side table next to his hospital bed to buy tickets for a B52s concert, fully expecting he would be released from hospital and better in time to go. Somehow he *was* better enough to be released from the hospital and attend the concert.

Over the summer of 1998, a giant dust storm blew over Dallas from Mexico. Bruce's lung function dropped so far that he would need a lung transplant to survive.

Bruce was displeased with the additional time and effort necessary to maintain his health after the decline in lung function brought on by the dust storm, but he didn't let that stop him. He convinced his bosses to let him move from Dallas to San Francisco (SF) and work remotely because the air was better in SF. Additionally, his lung function was so poor he no longer qualified for a lung transplant in Dallas. Standards were different in different parts of the country, and if he wanted to get a transplant in SF, it was still possible.

Bruce relocated to SF around Thanksgiving in 1998 and I followed in June 1999. My return to SF was partially based on being close to Bruce again but, truth be told, it was also largely driven by the dot com economy and a desire to be close to my family, who lived just outside of SF. In February 1999 Bruce surprised me with a marriage proposal. I knew the romantic thing to do would be to say yes right then and there, but when the man asking is basically dying, things move a little more slowly.

I prayed and I thought, and I asked the Universe for direction. What I heard was clear. I should go for it. Get Bruce to sign up for a lung transplant and then marry him. The Universe told me if I gave thanks for the transplant even before its physical arrival, everything would work out.

It did. Bruce and I married in January 2000. His call from the transplant center came in October 2000. About a week after his successful operation, we relocated to an apartment adjacent to the hospital where we lived for about six weeks so we could be close to care in case of an emergency. I told the Universe I wanted to be home with a healthy and healing Bruce by Christmas. We were released to go home on December 24, 2000.

To this day, I know it was my gratitude that carried the ball over the line and delivered that transplant for Bruce. While a lot of people thought I was crazy, my inner knowing and my constant thanking of the Universe for something that was yet to be delivered was what gave Bruce his transplant and led to many happy memories of our married life.

OBSTACLES AND SOLUTIONS TO GRATITUDE

"Feeling gratitude and not expressing it is like wrapping a present and not giving it." — William Arthur Ward

The opposite of gratitude is entitlement — taking things for granted. It is especially disturbing to know that by at least some metrics, entitlement is on the rise in the US.

Some of the most entitled people are narcissists. A narcissist is someone who has an excessive interest in or admiration of himself or herself. An inflated sense of self is a major obstacle to genuine gratitude. If a person is narcissistic, they will not express true gratitude because in their minds, they are deserving of greatness.

Jean Twenge is an American Psychologist and professor at San Diego State University. Keith Campbell is an American Social Psychology professor at the University of Georgia and an expert in narcissism. Twenge and Campbell reported in their book *The Narcissism Epidemic: Living in the Age of Entitlement*, that entitlement increased by approximately 30 percent in a fifteen-year period within the subgroups of children, adolescents, and young adults. The trend is not good.

Humility is another habit to develop that supports the cultivation of gratitude. Humble people spend less time defending themselves, and thus have more energy to spend on other people. Humility is a difficult virtue to cultivate. The intersection of humility and job hunting can be difficult to navigate. Humility is a doorway to gratitude.

There's another balance you must develop as a job hunter — a balance between being humble and being proud. Most people looking for a job struggle with this. I did have one colleague a long time ago who didn't struggle. "My favorite thing to do is look for and interview for a job. I know myself really well, and I love talking to new people about what I can do." He was in sales, as you might imagine. For everyone else I've known this balance can be tough.

This balance comes into play in several ways during a job hunt. First, it comes up when crafting a resumé and cover letters. Second, it comes up during the interview process. And third, it can come up while the employer checks references.

While developing a habit of humility surely has Adam II virtues, working on a humble habit can feel misaligned for active job seekers. It's not effective for job candidates to be overly humble. Overly humble candidates are unlikely to stand out and get job offers. Overly humble candidates aren't good for hiring organizations either, because the organization may get a reduced picture of what the candidate brings to the job.

It can be very hard to represent yourself well, especially as you start your job hunt. Knowing what to say to look capable, experienced, and confident but not cocky can be tricky. Reach out and find some help — maybe a personal friend or a prior colleague to help. Many job hunters find it worthwhile to hire professional help to ensure they are presenting their candidacy in an attractive way. Be honest and objective about your value as you manifest your new job.

GRATITUDE AS FUEL

"A grateful heart is a magnet for miracles." — Jane Fuller

Imagine using a new fuel to power yourself. Instead of fueling your body with proteins, carbs and fats, what if you fueled yourself with gratitude? While clearly good nutrition is important, I think it is worth considering making gratitude a fuel for your day.

It is possible to incorporate gratitude into almost any moment, purely by noticing what's around you. When you notice the dishes are dirty, you can be reminded of the meal you just ate. When you notice the flowers in the garden, you can be reminded of the lovely weather and gifts from Mother Nature. Notice the pile of work on your desk and you can feel blessed to have work to do. Gratitude tilts your interpretation of something about life to be a positive one, focused on what is versus what is not.

By making gratitude a running current through your day, your internal narrative will be one of abundance. Living your day using gratitude as your fuel means you are creating a constant framing of life towards the positive. I try to live my life where gratitude is like a low volume soundtrack that plays from sunrise to bedtime. By making moments of gratitude all day long, I am keeping my energy in a positive, receiving place — just right for receiving wonderful things like new friends and opportunities.

Our society is very money-motivated right now and many people are very fixated on material wealth. It is perfectly fine to want wealth; however, too much focus on the *wanting* can be unconstructive because you become too focused on what you don't have. Too much focus on the *wanting* takes away from the healing and attracting power of gratitude. Because you receive what you focus on, focusing on the wanting can lead to more and more wanting. This is not what you want to do.

For the remainder of today, and all of tomorrow, try making that gratitude soundtrack play in the background. In your free moments, look around and notice something to give thanks for. It doesn't have to be big. Get creative and have fun with this. If you break a glass, give thanks you still have another one. If your coworker is noisy, put on your headphones and be thankful for how well they work. Make being thankful a part of your day. The focus will make you a very kind and positive person to be around.

ADAPTATION AND GRATITUDE

"Gratitude turns what we have into enough." — Aesop

Adaptation is the nemesis of gratitude. We are all hard wired to adapt. Adaptation is the process of getting used to something and then taking it for granted. In the 1970s, only 13 percent of people thought air conditioning was a necessary feature in their car. Now some 40 percent plus of people think air conditioning is a necessary feature. Would you buy a new cell phone if it didn't have a camera? You would have ten years ago but now we are used to great cameras in our phones. That's adaptation.

Part of the trap of adaptation is that our enthusiasm about positive experiences tends to wane over time. Imagine finding a new restaurant with a dish you particularly love. The first time you have it, you just love the taste of this special dish. The second time you have the dish you enjoy it too. But odds are that the third or fourth time you order that special dish, it brings less joy than the first time. The emotional appeal of things that become more abundant or regular decreases over time.

There is a spiritual technique to address the trap of adaptation. Gratitude is the answer. If we remind ourselves to notice the good things we have in life regularly and to be thankful for them, we can push back against our natural tendency towards adaptation.

What kinds of adaptations have you made in your life? If you've changed jobs, you have adapted. If you've moved, you have adapted.

After my husband Bruce had his stroke and became disabled, I adapted to being a single mother. Even in the face of terrible and unforeseen circumstances, we cope and we adapt. It is important to remain strong and grateful whatever comes.

JOB CRAFTING

"If you don't have the best of everything, make the best of everything you have." — Erik Russell

Another way to approach the step of Thanks is job crafting. Job Crafting was originally described by professors Amy Wrzesniewski from Yale University and Jane E. Dutton from the University of Michigan in an article published in the Academy of Management

Review. Job crafting is the activity of redefining the work you do to increase your satisfaction with it. It is a proven way of feeling better about your job.

Job crafting takes a different approach to manifesting a new job by focusing on the present instead of the future. Even if you are desperate for a new job and hate the one you have, there are good reasons to learn about this technique.

We know that the premise of the law of attraction is that the Universe *will bring you more of what you have versus what you lack*. Focusing on lack is a losing strategy. If instead, you focus on the good things that you already have, the Universe will hear that call and deliver more good things. Job crafting is about gratitude and positivity, both powerful forces in the manifesting arena.

Sometimes it's impractical or unlikely that the perfect job will appear at the moment you want it. For example, if your industry goes through budgeting activities at certain times of the year, it may be that the perfect opening will come about after the money is funded. While there is always serendipity, we do live in a physical world with cycles, momentum, and other people. We often have to recognize that our perfect job isn't there…yet.

It may be that for you to get the job you want, you need to take a class, develop new skills, or meet new people, all of which could take time. Job crafting is an excellent step to take *in parallel* with your current work to manifest your new job. It can boost your mood while the Universe prepares the path to your new job.

I think of job crafting like adding stepping stones in my garden. It is helpful to have stones to step on when you walk; they keep one's feet out of the mud and dirt.

To job craft, examine your current job with a lens you haven't used in the past. Instead of focusing on the things in your job you want to change or escape from, focus on what is positive about your job. Sometimes this takes a little creativity to look at things in very different ways.

If you are presently working, please add the activity on job crafting to your activity list. If you are not presently working, read the activity and decide if there is value in doing it.

While we as a culture do a great job of giving thanks at Thanksgiving and religious holidays, many of us overlook the importance of giving thanks. This is not a mistake to make. Giving thanks is a critical part of the Manifestation Wheel. Don't cut corners. Give thanks consistently and the Universe will take note.

THANK
ACTIVITIES

COUNTING BLESSINGS

"When I started counting my blessings, my whole life turned around." — Willie Nelson

There's a wonderful TED talk by A. J. Jacobs about giving thanks. Jacobs decides that he wants to give thanks to everyone who played a part in providing him with his morning coffee. He begins with thanking the trucker who transported the coffee, and then the people who paved the road the trucker drove on. Watching his talk, you quickly begin to understand that it might not be possible within an entire lifetime to thank everyone who played a part in delivering that coffee.

In this activity, you are going to make a list of the blessings you have received in your journal. While the list could theoretically go on forever like Jacobs', it doesn't need to. In this step, you are reminding yourself and the Universe that you understand how many wonderful things you have received and that you are thankful for all of them.

Begin making your list. You don't need to go into detail, just enough so that you know what you are talking about. If you are stuck, look around the room you are in and find things you like to say thank you for. For your first pass at this activity, I recommend working on quantity versus quality. Instead of thanking everyone concerned, think more broadly. One way to do this is to think of your morning and imagine going through your day and giving thanks for all the things that come along in a typical day.

Probably, you can come up with 25 things. You might even come up with 50 or 100. If you get to a hundred, that's usually a good place to stop. At this point re-read your list. Undoubtedly you will think of a number of more things you are thankful for as you go through it and you can add those to the end.

Counting your blessings this way is an excellent way to kick-start the Thank step of the Manifestation Wheel.

STEPS:

1. Make a list of all the things you can think of to say thank you for.
2. When you run out, keep going using your environment, your memory, or whatever you need.

GRATITUDE JOURNALING

"The more one forgets himself — by giving himself to a cause to serve or another person to love — the more human he is and the more he actualizes himself." — Viktor E. Frankl

Great thinkers from the beginning of time have reminded us about how feeling gratitude is a wonderful thing to do, both for ourselves and for others. While there are numerous ways to show gratitude and express thanks, the gratitude journal is the most frequently recommended tool to create a habit of cultivating gratitude.

In his book, *Gratitude Works!*, Robert Emmons shares the results of numerous different studies done over time looking at which gratitude journaling habits produce the best results. Emmons recommends a 21-day get-started program to develop strong gratitude journaling habits.

His recommendations are well researched and straightforward, and I would encourage you to take up his 21 day program. A three week program is enough to get the gratitude ball rolling, and as we have discussed, there are numerous good physical and mental health benefits you can expect from developing gratitude. For our purposes, we are going to take more of a down and dirty approach.

Emmons writes that there are three essentials of writing in gratitude journals: scarcity, surprise, and specificity. Let's look at each of those.

Scarcity is the idea that when people think a positive event is about to end, they are more likely to appreciate it and try to get the most out of what remains of the event. Imagine going on vacation. A couple of days before the end of the vacation, you pay more attention to how much fun you are having on the vacation. This is the idea of scarcity.

Surprise matters in writing a gratitude journal entry because it is a driver of emotional intensity. Good or bad, when something is surprising, it is more memorable. I recently surprised my mother with a birthday cake. Because she wasn't expecting it, she was particularly thankful.

The last essential for gratitude journal writing is **specificity**. Specificity is important because the truth is in the details. Which statement contains more gratitude, "I am thankful my mother cooked me dinner," or "My mom cooked me my favorite dinner — tacos"? Including the details does a better job of articulating *why* you are thankful.

❧

For this activity, you are going to write at least five gratitude entries in your journal for things that have happened within the last week. You should write at least one for each essential elements of scarcity, surprise, and specificity.

Here are three examples:

Scarcity

"I am thankful for getting a chance to work with Joe in shipping. He is leaving for a new job next week, and if I hadn't had the time to work with him Thursday on our new process, I wouldn't have had the chance to meet him. Joe is a great guy; he had lots of good ideas and our company will miss him."

Surprise

"To my surprise, my son, who is never ready on time, was actually ready to leave for school on time this morning. Because he was on time, I was on time, and the whole day went better. I am thankful for his timeliness."

Specificity

"I am thankful for my most recent haircut. Jeanne did a great job and got the blonde highlights just right, the length perfect, and the shaggy ends the way I like them. After seeing Jeanne, I feel radiant and ready for anything."

Repeat this activity of writing five or more gratitude entries at least twice a week until you complete the first turn of the Manifestation

Wheel. Emmons points out that people can tire of gratitude journaling. It is important to keep it fresh and interesting. Writing only twice a week won't feel like a burden. It will start the ball rolling toward developing an attitude of gratitude and a practice of being more appreciative.

STEPS:

1. Write in your gratitude journal twice a week for at least three weeks.
2. Write five entries and make sure at least one entry focuses on each of the following: scarcity, surprise, and specificity.

A Favorite Place

"Life is too short to be living somebody else's dream."
— Hugh Heffner

In this activity, you are going to draw a picture of yourself in one of your favorite places. Choose a place that is meaningful to you — the forest, the beach, your room, a lake — wherever you feel completely relaxed.

Put as much detail into your drawing as you can. Make the trees tall, the ocean blue, and add flowers, streams, rocks, books, or whatever makes you happy. Don't hesitate to use lots of color to make your drawing beautiful.

As you add elements to your picture, think about the details and how much you like that they are a part of your scene. This picture of a favorite place is a means for you to notice, create, and give thanks for each of the different elements in your picture that makes that place so very special. If you are drawing trees, notice the leaves or the needles on the trees, and think about how they would feel if you could touch them. Give thanks for everything in the picture.

STEPS:

1. Draw a very specific and detailed picture of one of your favorite places. Fill it with as much detail as you can.
2. Next, use the picture as a way to find things to be grateful for, using all the details themselves as points of gratitude as you draw and then contemplate your drawing.

Job Crafting

*"The primary cause of unhappiness is never the situation
but your thoughts about it."*
— Eckhart Tolle

This activity is designed for people who are looking for a new job who have one presently. If you don't have a job at the moment, or this activity doesn't resonate with you, jump ahead to the next section.

Job crafting involves taking a fresh look at your work and thinking about it in a new way. Essentially, it is a reframing of your job that helps to see value in the work you are doing today. The purpose in this activity is not to eliminate your desire for a new job, but to better understand what you value. Job crafting can have the effect of making you see more meaning and purpose in what you are doing now, and to attract work with more meaning and purpose into your future.

Job manifesting can take time, and jobs don't always arrive the moment you planned. One benefit of job crafting while you are looking for a job is it helps to build energy related to your job hunt in a very positive way. Because of the law of attraction, job crafting to focus on the positives of the job you have now can help to attract a new job.

Here are some potential benefits you might receive from job crafting:
- Improving your satisfaction and enjoyment from what you do at work.
- Bringing in more energy and enthusiasm to your work.
- By improving skills, encouraging personal development.

The first step in job crafting is to decide where you get your primary pleasure from your work. "But I don't get pleasure from my job; that's why I want a new one," you might say. Certainly that may be true, but it is often possible to find something positive even about a job you plan to leave. This activity is about looking at the positive while you wait for your new job.

Work is an energy exchange. That energy exchange comes from many different types of energy. Three main types of energy exchange at work are task content, relationships, and purpose.

Task content involves the way things are done, using skills you already have to generate better results. For example, a friend of mine is a natural organizer. She takes joy from bringing her organizational and communication skills to the office to bring projects to launch. For her, job crafting is the recognition that her work is meaningful. It showcases her strengths and is something she is naturally good at.

Some people find tremendous meaning in their **relationships**. Job crafting with a focus on relationships is for people that find meaning in meeting people and helping them grow. Often, excellent managers derive meaning from relationships.

Purpose is an important element of work. Purpose can be at the organization level or at the individual level. For example, a dentist office could have a purpose to improve oral health in the community. A family law lawyer might have a purpose to help families achieve a greater sense of peace. Job crafting around the idea of purpose would mean heightening the importance of purpose in the way you approach your job.

STEPS:

1. For this activity, reflect upon your job and think about which of these three forms of energy exchange is the *most important for you.*
2. When you have identified which area: task content, relationships or purpose, write that down in your journal.
3. Rest in the feeling of what you do find satisfying or enjoyable about the job you have now.

Here is an example of Step 2:

"***Relationships****. What I love about my job is that as a manager, I have an opportunity to talk to my team about their problems and how to fix them. It's a chance for me to empathize with people who are often less experienced than I am and share with them my tips and techniques to solve problems. I like to listen to what they need and do what I can to provide what they need, whether it's a call to HR, approval to take a class, or help with a client call. I made a difference in this job by growing people and supporting strong internal and client relationships."*

The purpose of this activity is not to persuade you to stop looking for a new job, but to help you *rest in the feeling* that there is something about the job you have right now that is valuable and worthwhile. Feeling valuable at work is helpful to attract a new job.

RECEIVE

RECEIVE

"If you want the whole thing, the gods will give it to you.
But you must be ready for it."
— Joseph Campbell

R eceive is another word for accept or acceptance. In the case of manifesting a new job, it's the step you've been working towards all along. This step helps and reminds you to be prepared and ready to receive your new job when it comes along. Without Receive, you cannot complete your process. Receiving can be uncomfortable for all of us sometimes. Learning to do it well is a necessary skill for this job search and for your life.

It can help to remember that the Universe seeks balance; it is the natural way of things. We have day and night, high tides and low tides, hot and cold. In the same way, the Universe must have givers to have receivers. And we must at different times be givers, and yes, receivers.

It's important to keep in mind that we all must give to receive. Our parents taught us this when we were children and it is no less true today. So, part of our receiving journey will be learning to give. If you want to receive a new job, be a giving person.

Receiving starts with declaring you are receiving. It is important to "own" the feeling that you receive as a matter of course. Consider yourself a receiver and notice how much you receive.

Stay positive and have faith. It is easy to feel like giving up after working hard on the previous steps, but you must maintain focus. Sometimes you must hold the rudder for a little while until your ship arrives in port.

When I feel low, questioning if what I am hoping to receive will ever arrive, I remind myself of something a co-worker said to me years ago. "When you ask the Universe for something, there are only two answers. "Yes," and "not yet, something even better is coming your way." This lifts my spirits and returns my hope.

THE THREE TYPES OF GIVING

"Giving is better than receiving because giving starts the receiving process."
— Jim Rohn

There are three ways the Universe asks us to give. The first is to give anonymously to the Universe in general. This can take the form of giving to organizations or religious groups. This type of giving is very important because you are not seeking anything specific in return. This kind of giving is a giving of faith. It is a giving that demonstrates confidence that the gift itself carries positive spiritual energy. Know that with this kind of giving, you are opening the door to being on the receiving side of numerous gifts — gifts even beyond your imagination. For example, letting another car go ahead of you in the parking lot is a simple way to give anonymously. By letting a stranger go first, you are giving them a tiny gift of moving ahead of you, and thus opening the door to more receiving energy.

The second way to give is to yourself. In today's busy world, it is not uncommon for people to get off balance and fail to give to themselves and take care of themselves properly. "Put on your oxygen mask first," as the saying goes. We will not have the energy we need if we fail on a regular basis to take care of ourselves.

While it's certainly possible to lean into adrenaline to get through a crisis and put giving to yourself to the side, it's not smart to keep doing this over and over. It's imperative to take care of yourself, including having time to relax, to keep up with your health and medical needs and to sleep. If you are not taking care of yourself, the Universe may recognize that this isn't a good time to receive a job and hold back. Don't allow that to happen.

Giving to someone else is the third way to give. Doesn't it feel wonderful to bring someone a gift they enjoy? Keep in mind that giving to someone else doesn't just mean a physical gift, but any gift of your time, talent, or treasure. It is not necessary to have money to give to others, but it is necessary to make time and energy to share with them.

Giving brought me two assignments overseas. In the early 1990s, I worked for an international consulting company. I had a job where I traveled almost weekly all over the US, going to meetings and supporting the partners and executives of our company and of our clients. I loved traveling, and I wondered if I could transform my job to allow me to travel overseas.

I gave a lot at this time in my life. Not only did I give my all at work, doing an excellent job for my projects and clients, but I also gave a lot at home. I flew so much for work at that time I had accrued more frequent flier miles than I could use myself. One Christmas, I gifted my parents with complimentary tickets to Europe that came from my frequent flier miles. I trained new people at work. I tipped everyone generously when I traveled. I was a giver.

When we came to a break on my most active client's project, I took a chance. I left one of the partners of the consulting company a voicemail message saying I was interested in overseas assignments, and could he please contact me if something came up. Ten days later he called me with an offer to go to New Zealand for two to six months to support a client project. A week later I was on a plane.

I returned to California when that assignment finished and started working with a new team. A couple of months later an opportunity to work overseas in London came up and I was asked to go. I had a wonderful time working in our London office and traveling to Europe and the Middle East from my new home base.

My giving to the Universe, myself and others, was rewarded with receiving multiple wonderful overseas assignments. I am so thankful that I had these opportunities.

DECLARE YOU ARE RECEIVING

"For it is in giving that we receive." — St. Francis of Assisi

To receive, declare that you are receiving. Not just receiving the new job, but also all the little things you are receiving along the way. Tell others about the great things you receive — like a greeting card from your Mom, a phone call from an old friend, or a cookie from the shopkeeper. This kind of activity is heard by the Universe. As like attracts like, the more you notice and experience the feeling of receiving, the more you will receive.

I received the man of my dreams.

At 5'10" tall, finding a partner taller than me has not always been easy. Add to that more criteria that I wanted to find in a man like: kind, smart, funny, close by, educated, shared interests, ethical and available, and the options grow thinner still. All my life, I had been dreaming of a tall, handsome gentleman to sweep me off my feet and in 2015 I found him.

I spent Christmas 2014 partner-less. I had split up in November with a boyfriend I had been seeing after I came to the realization that he was definitely not the one for me.

On a lark, I decided to set up a profile on eHarmony. I view online dating as an excellent way of telling the Universe you are serious about finding someone, and open to how that will come to be, online or offline. After about two weeks, I had received very few messages and I was still feeling down.

I decided in early January not to let the lack of attention bother me, but instead to get busy and send out some messages to interesting men. I selected about 10 profiles and waited. I heard back from one man: Scott.

We met for coffee about a week later and I was instantly entranced. Not only was Scott tall (6'4"), but he was a geotechnical engineer who loved nature, camping, and singing. Scott played guitar and had a voice like velvet. He was everything I had dreamed of in a man.

Guess what? Scott was crazy about me! I came to realize that Scott had also dreamed of having a very romantic and committed partner. He had been married before, but he and his wife did not have a passionate relationship like we did. Scott and I were very blessed to have found each other and had so many wonderful times together.

I was so blessed to have received this wonderful man for the time we had together. Scott passed in 2021. His spirit lives on in me now.

THE TIME TO RECEIVE

"God never gives someone a gift they are not capable of receiving. If he gives us the gift of Christmas, it is because we all have the ability to understand and receive it." — Pope Francis

Receiving can be difficult because you may be tired at this point. If you have been working hard at turning the Manifestation Wheel, receiving can be hard because you want to receive that job offer immediately and it just doesn't come. If this happens you must have faith.

While all of the steps in the Manifestation Wheel are at least somewhat interpersonal in nature, the step of Receive is the most social. As you begin to turn the wheel, the early steps of Release and Create, which both heavily focus on internal work, give way to Thank and Receive, where the external energy is elevated. Instead of being alone in a spotlight, the full lights have turned on and the stage includes other people. In this phase, you should envision yourself in a web of energy, connected to friends, family, neighbors, and former and future colleagues. Energy passes from person to person, continuously moving and changing.

The day will come when what was once a possibility becomes an opportunity and you are in a place to receive. Congratulations! This is what you have been working for.

Rarely, but sometimes, turners of the Manifestation Wheel question "but is this the right job?" Usually it is. If you've been serious about following the steps of the Manifestation Wheel, most jobs that are poor fits will have fallen out of the running, leaving the jobs you are offered, the ones with a spiritual fit.

Occasionally, the Manifestation Wheel can appear to get you the wrong job. If you find yourself in this odd predicament, hold on. It will likely be a bumpy ride, but it will sort itself out in time.

One year I was pushing hard to find a new job and I had leads I was working on for several different jobs. All required a similar set of skills, but the emphasis of each job was a bit different. One was a project manager role, one a strategic and execution marketing manager role, and one was as a subject matter expert. Curiously, two leads were for the same pharmaceutical company, but through different intermediary agencies. I was applying to two jobs that were on the same team, but nobody knew that except me. The third job was at a financial institution where two of my friends worked.

What happened was very strange. I was not offered the pharmaceutical subject matter expert job, which was the job I felt I would be best at. No reason was given why they didn't want me for the subject matter expert job, which was frustrating, but sometimes that's how it goes. About a week later I was offered the other job at the pharma company, the project manager job. Of the three jobs, this was the one I felt was only a mediocre fit.

About a day before I started this contracting role, I told my new boss at the intermediary agency that things could be a bit weird, as we would be meeting people on my first day who I had interviewed with for the subject matter expert job. My new boss was surprised, but it seemed like everything was fine, so I started the pharmaceutical project manager job. As expected, the pharma team was surprised to see me as I started the work. Fortunately, they seemed happy with my fit in this role.

Within one week, I was getting the feeling that the job was not a good fit for me. The company culture was a challenge, and the expectations for the role changed significantly once the work started. The pharma company was trying to take on many changes quickly, in part evidenced by all this hiring they were doing. I was unhappy.

Two weeks later, the financial company where my friends worked called. Whatever obstacle they previously had, disappeared and they wanted me to start as soon as possible. I am not one to quit a commitment, but this was a very particular situation where I knew I was not going to provide the pharmaceutical company with what they needed. I knew that things would continue going downhill for me at the pharma company, and I was confident I would fit in at the financial company. I gave notice to the pharma company and accepted at the financial services company.

It's hard to make sense of this sequence of events. Why did all this happen, and happen the way it did? There is no answer. Reflecting on those events, perhaps I should not have accepted the pharma project manager job, but who's to say really? In the end, I found a job I really liked, and even had a chance to work with some personal friends and make more friends.

Most of the time, when you arrive at the step of Receive, it will be clear what you should do. If it's not that clear, lean into your intuition and be patient.

Receiving can be tough even though it sounds easy. Leaning into the feeling of gratitude helps. Positivity is a must; sometimes patience is required. The next chapter covers some activities to help you practice receiving.

RECEIVE
ACTIVITIES

RECEIVE ALL DAY

"Everything comes to us that belongs to us if we create the
capacity to receive it."
— Rabindranath Tagore

Your first activity in the Receive step will have you take an entire day to focus on receiving. From dawn to bedtime, practice receiving all day. Notice every kindness and thoughtfulness you receive that day. Every time you speak to another person, notice their care, interest, love or attention that they pay to you. The goal is to bring the receiving of energy from everyone you encounter top of mind.

As you practice this receiving, say to yourself silently, "I receive. I am blessed today." You are boosting your receiving powers and attracting more receiving by focusing on it.

Make the effort to ask for at least one thing today. Perhaps it is a ride to a meeting, or for someone to pass the sugar, or even something bigger like inviting someone new to lunch. As you ask, imagine the person does what you have asked and you are receiving.

At the end of the day, write in your journal about the many things you received. Include what happened when you asked for something.

STEPS:

1. Focus on the things you receive today.
2. When you find one, tell yourself: "I receive. I am blessed today!"
3. Write in your journal about the many things you received to make them stick in your memory.

RECEIVING BOARD

"The visionary starts with a clean sheet of paper,
and re-imagines the world." — Malcolm Gladwell

Begin to practice receiving by making a collage called a "Receiving Board." It can be physical or digital, but I do recommend a large physical collage. A large physical collage has the advantage of being something sizable and graphic that you can look at frequently when you are done. If you work better digitally, just make sure to print out, in color and large format, what you create.

First, gather some images of things you have already received. You may choose exact images, like a snapshot of your spouse or representative pictures like a magazine picture of a couple. Either type of image will work because both exemplify the idea of "spouse" in your subconscious mind.

Only choose positive images. The Receiving Board is, like all of the activities, a way of putting your energy in motion to draw in more of what you want.

The Receiving Board is similar to a Vision Board. A Vision Board is a collage of images of things you imagine in your future. What distinguishes a Receiving Board from a Vision Board is that the Receiving Board *also* includes images of things you have *already* received.

After you have collected images of things you have already received, move on to collecting images of things you *will* receive. These images of what you will receive can be big or small. I do recommend that some be small, like a sunny day or a nice meal, because if you overload your board with images of big asks like race cars and mansions, your board will feel more like a vision board and our activity here is to make a Receiving Board.

At least two or three of the Receiving Board images for the future should be things you associate with work. While it doesn't technically matter (because your life is all one), include the idea of work since this effort is to manifest a new job. You might include a picture of an office, a map of where you want to work, or an image of a certificate or diploma. You could include an image of yourself doing something you might do for work, like working on the computer or talking on the phone. The work part doesn't have to be a dominant portion of your Receiving Board, but it should be included.

Receiving Boards can also have text on them, so if there are words you like and want to put on the board, go right ahead. In my experience, it works best if words are added to the Receiving Board like spices are added to spaghetti sauce. Visuals remain dominant, but a few words can be nice. The human mind is very visual. By focusing on images instead of words, it will resonate highly with your subconscious, bringing energy and power with it.

Once you have a pile of images ready to go, lay them out on your Receiving Board. Mix them up and make them pretty. There are no rules about how to place the images on the board. Do include, as mentioned above, a few things already received, at least one small thing you will receive, and a couple of things about work.

The Receiving Board makes use of the illusion of time. While we perceive past, present, and future as separate, all times are really one. Your brain has a hard time distinguishing real from imagined, and so in this single collage, you are tricking your brain into thinking that everything is already received, because your brain recognizes that some of the images are really already received.

When your Receiving Board is complete, post it on a wall where you will see it several times a day. By seeing it several times a day, your subconscious will soak in the energy from these images and your work, focusing your thoughts on what you have and will receive.

STEPS:

1. Collect images of things you have received already.
2. Collect images of things you want to receive (at least two of which are work related).
3. Put them all on your receiving board.
4. Place the board where you can see it and let your subconscious soak it up.

THE LOVE I HAVE RECEIVED

"And so I have come to understand that strength, inner strength, comes from receiving love as much as it comes from giving it." — Donald Miller

All of us are the recipients of love. Love is at the center of our human experience. Love is inexhaustible, endless and infinite. It is central to our beings to give and to receive love.

In this activity, you will focus on the love that you have received, deeply appreciating that love, and observing different aspects of it, strengthening your receiving muscles.

Bring to mind someone from whom you have received tremendous love. It might be a parent, a partner, a teacher, a child, a relative, or a dear friend. The person might be alive or dead. It is important that this person is a real person who you had a close relationship to in real life, past or present. Select someone whose love for you stands out; ideally someone whose love exceeded your expectations.

Take five or ten minutes to deeply reflect on this person and the love that they shared with you. As you remember your relationship, go through the five W's and the H question:

- When did you know them? What was going on in your life?
- Who were they to you? What was your relationship?
- Where were you? What sorts of places did you visit together?
- What was your relationship about?
- Why was it such a positive relationship?
- How did they express their love?

In your journal, write a paragraph or two about this person, and how you received their love. Focus on the feeling of what it felt like to receive love. This is a good activity to repeat remembering different people. Reviving this feeling of receiving love will encourage you to show love to others, and to remember the feeling of receiving.

STEPS:

1. Bring to mind someone from whom you have received tremendous love.
2. Deeply reflect on this person and the love that they shared with you. As you remember your relationship, go through the five W's and the H questions.
3. In your journal, write about this person focusing on what it felt like to receive the love from this person.

BATHE IN THE FOREST, GROUND YOURSELF IN THE EARTH

"It's your road and yours alone. Others may walk it with you, but no one can walk it for you." — Rumi

Manifesting a new job is easier if you solicit the power of nature to help. Research over the last century has proven that by spending time in nature and grounding ourselves in the energy of the earth, we make improvements in numerous aspects of our physical well-being. The final activity in turning the Manifestation Wheel involves going outside.

The Japanese practice of shinrin-yoku involves spending time in nature, in a forest if available, to just "be." A study sponsored by the Environmental Protection Agency found that the average American spends 93 percent of his or her time indoors. A study published in 2010 found that young adults who spent 15 to 20 minutes walking and viewing forests experienced lower concentrations of cortisol, lower pulse rates, and lower blood pressure than control subjects who spend an equivalent amount of time in a city area. Researchers are continuing to look at forest bathing to better understand how and why the benefits of being in nature are so high.

Forest bathing can be a still or a moving experience. It is especially peaceful and meditative to walk in the forest, but it can also be very nurturing to sit down and be still. Either method is beneficial for your health, but adding walking to your time in the forest has the benefit of including physical movement.

I like to combine my time forest bathing with "earthing." Earthing is a form of connecting one's physical body to the earth's natural magnetic frequency. Our ancestors spent generations where their physical bodies were frequently in touch with the earth. Now, however, we spend very little time during the day physically touching the earth. Researchers are studying the effect of grounding the physical body in the earth's magnetic frequency, either through a very low tech method like walking barefoot or sitting on the lawn, or through a more technology-enhanced method, like a mat connected to the grounding wires in an electric outlet in a high rise apartment. There is very promising evidence that grounding oneself in the earth's energy can reduce inflammation in the body. Because many of us have excessive inflammation in the body, earthing can be especially helpful to our physical bodies.

It is well worth a trip to the forest for this activity. Alternatively, choose a natural place with dirt or rocks on the ground where you can sit undisturbed for at least 30 minutes and start at the sitting part of the activity.

I recommend taking an hour for this activity if you can make the time.

ॐ

Start by walking in the forest or outdoors for at least 20 minutes. As you walk, look around and listen. Notice how the light comes through the trees. Notice the forest floor, and the flowers and plants. If there are sounds, listen to them and imagine the creatures that make those sounds. Think of your body as a great receiver of this experience and enjoy it.

It is very common as you begin this activity to find your mind drifting off into your world back home. That's natural. However, this is not a time to think about life outside the forest, your friends or your job hunt. It is a time to receive. If you have thoughts about life back home, notice them and let them drift away. Consider putting them on a cloud that drifts away to another part of the sky. They will come back later, but you don't need them right now.

As you think about receiving, think about how that is happening with all your senses. You are receiving through the five senses you learned about in school: touch, taste, sight, hearing and smell. Other senses that will grow as you do this activity: intuition and the sense of where your body is in space. As you forest bathe, your ability to pick up these subtle cues with your subconscious grows.

After walking about 20 minutes, sit down. Sit on the earth or a rock, or take off your shoes if you choose to sit on a bench. The goal is to put your physical body in touch with the earth's magnetic field so that you will receive the healing electro-magnetic energy of the earth. Once again, notice what's going on around you. I find it helpful to close my eyes from time to time, so that I can better focus on my non-visual senses. How many different birds can you hear? Is there a sound of a bee buzzing by? Recently during a forest visit, my intuition spoke to me and told me that somewhere off to my left there were a group of bugs, bees perhaps, buzzing around. Let your mind open and explore this natural place. Receiving the earth's energy and the energy of the forest is your only goal.

Twenty minutes after sitting in nature soaking up the earth's magnetic field, walk back to your starting place. Odds are that on the return walk, it will be much easier to focus on the forest than it was when you first arrived. Again, notice the sights, sounds, smells and even taste of the forest as you walk. Keep the thought of receiving in mind.

When you get back to your starting point, give thanks. Thank nature for the wonderful experience. This activity has elevated your sense of receiving. As like draws like, this feeling of receiving will help to draw your next job to you.

STEPS:

1. Start by walking in the forest or outdoors for at least 20 minutes. As you walk, look around, listen, and pay attention to receiving with all your senses.
2. Put your physical body in touch with the earth's magnetic field so that you will receive the healing electro-magnetic energy of the earth. Focus on your senses.
3. When you get back to your starting point, give thanks to nature of the experience of receiving its bounty.

WRAPPING UP

WRAPPING UP

*"Blessed is he who has found his work; let him ask no other blessedness,
he has a work, a life-purpose; he has found it and will follow it."*
— Thomas Carlyle

Now that you've worked your way through the Manifestation Wheel, you have lifted your getting-a-job energy to a place where you will be both more open and targeted in your job search. Well done!

Perhaps you are nearing the point of receiving and taking a job offer. Or, there's a chance that your next job is still coming into being on the physical plane. One tool I rely on to help me when the job is in the process of arriving but has not yet arrived is the Circle Of Influence.

THE CIRCLE OF INFLUENCE

"Live out of your imagination, not your history." — Steven Covey

In his book, *The Seven Habits of Highly Effective People*, Steven Covey offers many great words of wisdom. One of my favorites is his illustration of the Circle of Influence and Circle of Control. This framework is essentially a means to map thoughts and concerns and can be very helpful in many areas, including job hunts. These circles are elastic, and change with circumstances and time.

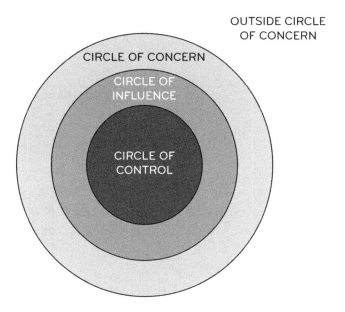

The Circle of Influence is a set of concentric circles. The largest circle is called the Circle of Concern; the middle circle is the Circle of Influence; and the smallest circle in the middle is the Circle of Control.

The Circle of Concern is where you map things you are concerned about but that you have no ability to influence and no ability to control. You may be worried about genocide in other parts of the world or whether you son can hold down his new job. Both fit in the Circle of Concern because you have no influence and no control over these situations even if you experience strong concern.

The Circle of Influence is where you map things you have some level of input on, but not complete control. College applications fit in this category. You have some degree of influence with grades, interviews, and application essays, but the final decision on whether you are accepted is not within your control. The Circle of Influence is dynamic and changeable. What is in your Circle of Influence now is probably different from what was in it a few years ago. For example, if you have children, as they grow up, more and more things move from the Circle of Control to the Circle of Influence. The Circle of Influence can contract or expand depending on your situation, your relationships, your training, and other forces.

The smallest circle is the Circle of Control. There's only so much each of us individually controls. You probably control what you eat for dinner and what time you go to bed. You don't have control over whether a new firm will hire you or whether your teenager will make his late night curfew.

It's perfectly normal to struggle with the Circle of Control. Most people have things they want to be in their Circle of Control but aren't. For example, you may want your children to try harder or achieve top marks, but that might not be in your Circle of Control. Your job search is one of those things that does not fall into the Circle of Control, so it's a perfect time to work with your attitudes and skills around this practice.

When I am struggling with an issue, I often step back and consider where my issues sit within these three circles. If the issue is in my Circle of Control, the good news is that I have power in the situation. If instead it is in the Circle of Influence, I have some sway over it, but not control. Many things sit in my Circle of Concern, and I must accept that there is nothing in my power to affect or change them.

When this happens, I take a few deep breaths. Usually I find this is a time for acceptance. For job hunts, sometimes I can think of something in my Circle of Influence to take action on, like calling someone or following up, but sometimes there is only acceptance. Many times when I have reached this stage, I find it helpful to call a friend and talk it out. Leaning on your support network can help reduce negative feelings of frustration or anxiety.

This framework has helped me countless times. Understanding what is in my Circle of Control and what is in my Circle of Influence is a balm for my nerves and helps me stay on track.

KEY CONCEPTS

Work has a purpose. Work is an expression of spirit. Let's go back to the GET PIE list so we can think anew about the reasons people work which may resonate with you differently now that you have gone through this book and opened up your ideas about work. There are at least six reasons why people work:

- **Growing**: The Challenges of Work, Growing From New Skills
- **Expressing**: Oneself From Your Place of True Self
- **Training**: Learning and Preparing For Something Else
- **Playing**: Making Work Feel Like Play
- **Interacting**: With Other People and Making the Lives of Others Better
- **Energizing**: Playing Your Part in the Flow of the Universe

Which ones now feel important in this job search? Which ones do you need more of in your life? What is your intuition about what you need for your next job to learn the lessons you need to learn? What feels satisfying and enjoyable to you? Take some time to think and feel your way through the list and make a note in your journal of what you learned.

Through your mindset and the actions you take, you can draw on invisible forces to attract a new job. By opening up your inner self, learning these skills, and practicing them, you can leverage your spirit to assist you in your job hunt. The way to do this is through the Manifestation Wheel. You are well versed in the Manifestation Wheel and you may look at this differently as a result. There are four steps in the Manifestation Wheel:

- Release
- Create
- Thank
- Receive

In the step of **Release**, you learned to let go of energy, particularly negative energy, and to put energy in motion. Your job hunt does not live in a silo; it is a part of your life that must live in balance with everything else. All parts of your life are related, including sour relationships, necessary self-care and time spent playing with friends. The Universe will not take your job hunt seriously and deliver a wonderful new job to you if you are harboring excessive negative energy which needs to be released. Now that you have worked with Release, how can you fit those practices into your life so that what you learned on your job hunt enriches your world?

Create is the second step. In the step of Create, you envisioned and crystalized your picture of what a wonderful job would look like. Create is the step where you directed and framed what you are looking for in a new job. While a conscious analysis of what you need in a job on the physical plane is important and necessary, the step of Create also integrates your intuition to focus your job hunting efforts in the right direction. The step of Create includes dreams and hope, and is a critical part of turning the Manifestation Wheel. Create has applications across your entire life — from work, to friendships, to creativity, to house hunting, to love, to your health and wellbeing. Take the time to choose some create practices you will do over and over as you move through your life.

Thank comes next. You spent time getting good at using gratitude as a healthy habit and an integral part of your success. Thanking includes a recognition that energy is in motion. It also puts the body and mind in a positive state for receiving more. Thanking may also include being thankful for the job you have as you transition to something new.

The fourth step is **Receive**. To prepare to receive a new job that is aligned with your spirit, you prepared to receive. Giving is important and so is receiving. Practice receiving by seeing energy in motion and taking it in.

Although these steps are described as sequential, once you work through them you will find you can be doing all of them in different parts and pieces at the same time. I think of this as "spinning" your Manifestation Wheel. It should be your goal, as you grow more comfortable with this method, to work on any and all steps that feel appropriate so that your Manifestation Wheel stays in motion. Staying limber at the Manifestation Wheel means that the next time you need something, you won't find yourself at the beginning again, but instead you will have skills and tools ready and waiting for you.

These are the steps to finding a spirit-fulfilling job. In combination with the necessary actions one must take at the physical level, including resumés, applications, phone calls and so forth, they will bring you a great job.

MORE EVIDENCE FOR MANIFESTING

Before I conclude, I want to share one more joyful story of manifesting something wonderful. Unfortunately, my husband Bruce was infertile. I knew this when we married, but I remained hopeful that someday we would find a way to have a child. We decided to try donor sperm. Because many people in my family, including myself, are born in December, I figured March would be a magic month for me. Although my doctor told me I had a one in four chance of getting pregnant with donor sperm, I got pregnant on my first try. Thank you, gods of March!

When I was pregnant, I heard many birth stories of women. A great many of them seemed to be about spending hours in painful labor and the difficulties of giving birth. During this time my Mom threw a party and I spoke to her friend Diane. Diane shared with me that she had given birth to three boys, and every time she went into labor, she delivered her son very quickly and easily. I consciously decided I would reject all the other stories about the long difficult births and focus on being like Diane.

I went about setting my dominant energy to be one expecting a fast and easy delivery. Consciously and subconsciously, I thought "I'm going to be like Diane. I will have an easy birth."

When people wanted to tell me stories about how long or challenging their process of giving birth was, I would nod and pretend to listen. But in my head I was thinking "My story will be similar to Diane's." What happened the day I gave birth? My labor came on so fast my girlfriend had to drive me to the hospital. My husband was a couple of hours away at a business meeting and couldn't drive home in time. When I arrived at the hospital, my labor proceeded so quickly, the emergency doctor began the delivery because my gynecologist had not arrived. There was no time to give me painkillers before active labor started. Fortunately, my husband and gynecologist arrived before my son did. My belief that I would have a labor like Diane came true for me, and my beautiful son was born in a fast and easy delivery.

There are a couple of points to this story. First, I had faith that I would have a child, faith that trying in March would prove effective, and faith that if I believed in a fast labor, I would have one. Second, I was courteous to everyone who shared a challenging birth story, but privately I didn't engage with that negative energy. I kept Diane's story top-of-mind, leaning into a cognitive availability bias to see things positively, that I could have a fast childbirth. This is an example of using a cognitive bias in a positive way. Thought control turns the Manifestation Wheel.

And if you are a Mom who had a difficult birth, I am not saying that you caused it. I just chose to take a very optimistic perspective during my pregnancy to make it go easier.

CONCLUSION

You've reached the end of the book, but not of the journey. What you have learned in these lessons are important tools and techniques for bringing a new job into your life. Perhaps, like the sun rising over the horizon, the new job has started to make its appearance, or perhaps it is still hours before dawn and the coming of the new job is not yet apparent.

Have faith. In reading this book and doing the activities, you are more aligned with what is in your heart and closer to attracting the right work for you.

This book explains how to approach bringing something wonderful — a great job — into your life, but the principles described here apply to many more areas than work. Your life is one big experience, and work is one part of it. Life is messy and filled with family and friends as well as houses, cars, joy and curiosity you experience, your clothes, the place you live, and even your relationships with the people you love. Apply the Manifestation Wheel framework to other parts of your life and see what happens.

I hope my references and stories have helped you to understand why I am confident that this approach will work for you. After eighteen plus jobs and considerable personal loss and hardship, I know from experience how critical it is to have a strong and spirit-aligned approach to your job hunt. You can do this too.

Thank you for letting me be your guide on this journey, and best wishes to you now and always. And if you want to "take a page from my book," remember, like I said that I wanted my birth to be like Diane's, you can say, "I want my job search to be like Michelle's."

Your life is a tapestry of experiences, including your work, your relationships, and your experiences. This process can be applied to your job hunt, and many other aspects of your life. Doing so will enrich your life in ways you never expected.

RESOURCES

CHAPTER 3

What Color Is Your Parachute? 2022: Your Guide to a Lifetime of Meaningful Work and Career Success
Richard N. Bolles

Land Your Dream Job: Join the 2% Who Make it Past Resumé Screening
Michael LaChance

Hired
George C. Murray

How to Enjoy Your Life and Your Job
Dale Carnegie

Self-Hypnosis: Key to your Inner Power
Gil Boyne

Self-Hypnosis and Other Mind Expanding Techniques
Charles Tebbetts

CHAPTER 5

The Paradox of Choice: Why More Is Less
Barry Schwartz

CHAPTER 6

The Happiness Advantage: How a Positive Brain Fuels Success in Work and Life
Shawn Achor

The Art of Healing: Uncovering Your Inner Wisdom and Potential for Self-Healing
Bernie S. Sigel, MD

RESOURCES

CHAPTER 7

The Road to Character
David Brooks

Finding Flow: The Psychology of Engagement with Everyday Life
Mihaly Csikszentmihalyi

CHAPTER 8

Gratitude Works!: A 21-Day Program for Creating Emotional Prosperity
Robert A. Emmons

The Narcissism Epidemic: Living in the Age of Entitlement
Jean Twenge and W. Keith Campbell

Wrzesniewski, Amy & Dutton, Jane. (2001). *Crafting a Job: Revisioning Employees as Active Crafters of Their Work.* Academy of Management Review. 26. 179-201. 10.2307/259118. The Academy of Management Review 26(2):179-201

Job Crafting: Shaping Your Job to Fit You Better
MindTools Content Team

How to Trust Your Vibes at Work and Let Them Work for You
Sonia Choquette

CHAPTER 9

My journey to thank all the people responsible for my morning coffee
A.J. Jacobs

CHAPTER 11

Forest Bathing' Is Great for Your Health. Here's How to Do It
Time Magazine

Park BJ, Tsunetsugu Y, Kasetani T, Kagawa T, Miyazaki Y. *The physiological effects of Shinrin-yoku (taking in the forest atmosphere or forest bathing): evidence from field experiments in 24 forests across Japan.* Environ Health Prev Med. 2010 Jan;15(1):18-26. doi: 10.1007/s12199-009-0086-9. PMID: 19568835; PMCID: PMC2793346.

Earthing: Health Implications of Reconnecting the Human Body to the Earth's Surface Electrons
Chevalier G, Sinatra ST, Oschman JL, Sokal K, Sokal P. Earthing: health implications of reconnecting the human body to the Earth's surface electrons. *J Environ Public Health.* 2012;2012:291541. doi:10.1155/2012/291541

CHAPTER 12

The 7 Habits of Highly Effective People
Stephen Covey

SUPPORTING CONTENT

What can you find at www.michellewalters.net?

At www.michellewalters.net you will find a plethora of supporting content for *An Alignment of Spirit: Finding Work You Love*.

This includes:
- Practice hypnosis recordings to open your mind
- A shareable copy of the first chapter
- Hypnosis recordings that pair with the activities in the book to help you reflect on and process those activities at the subconscious level
- Step summaries from several of the activities

Please visit www.michellewalters.net and take advantage of these helpful materials.

Made in the USA
Las Vegas, NV
19 August 2022